FALL OF HEAVEN

· · · · · ·

WHYMPER'S TRAGIC
MATTERHORN CLIMB

REINHOLD MESSNER

TRANSLATED BY BILLI BIERLING

LEGENDS AND LORE SERIES

MOUNTAINEERS
BOOKS

Mountaineers Books is the publishing division of The Mountaineers, an organization founded in 1906 and dedicated to the exploration, preservation, and enjoyment of outdoor and wilderness areas.

MOUNTAINEERS BOOKS

1001 SW Klickitat Way, Suite 201, Seattle, WA 98134
800.553.4453, www.mountaineersbooks.org

Printed in the United States of America
20 19 18 17   1 2 3 4 5

Copyeditor: Chris Dodge
Series design: Karen Schober
Layout: Jen Grable, Mountaineers Books
Cover and interior illustrations from *Scrambles Amongst the Alps* by Edward Whymper

Library of Congress Cataloging-in-Publication Data available on file.

Mountaineers Books titles may be purchased for corporate, educational, or other promotional sales, and our authors are available for a wide range of events. For information on special discounts or booking an author, contact our customer service at 800-553-4453 or mbooks@mountaineersbooks.org.

♻ Printed on recycled paper

MIX
Paper from
responsible sources
FSC **FSC® C005010**
www.fsc.org

ISBN (paperback): 978-1-68051-085-0
ISBN (ebook): 978-1-68051-086-7

CONTENTS

PROLOGUE

NO OTHER MOUNTAIN IN THE world has such distinct features as the Matterhorn. It appears inaccessible from all sides. What did the residents of the Swiss canton of Valais think or feel thousands of years ago, when they first set eyes on the mountain that locals to this day call Horu? Did they worry that avalanches or rocks would tumble down onto their pastures and destroy their livelihoods? Could they predict the weather in the mists gathering on its flanks? Or were they just too frightened to go anywhere near it?

The initial name given to this unique mountain is said to have been Mons Silvius. The Swiss philosopher and geologist Horace-Bénédict de Saussure, as well as the Schlagintweit brothers, who published a geological geography of the Alps in 1854, used the name Mont Cervin in their reports, and both noted 1682 as the first record of the names "Zermatt" and "Matterhorn."

When Saussure first passed through the Valtournenche Valley on his way to the southern base of the Matterhorn in 1789, he had no intention of climbing this awkward-looking mountain. Two years previously he had stood atop the highest mountain of the Alps, Mont Blanc. There he took barometer readings to establish the exact height of the peak.

In 1789 there was no route to the top of the Matterhorn, which rises gigantically into the sky over the wide pastures of Breuil. The triangular obelisk, looking as if it had been chiseled, was considered unscalable. Its ragged cliffs, too steep to allow snow to cling, would not allow even the thought of an ascent.

On his second trip to the Alps in 1792, Saussure started in Valtournenche, advanced to the Col de Saint-Théodule, and stayed there for three days to analyze the structure of the Matterhorn and determine its exact height. He collected rocks, plants, and insects, wondering how the glacier fleas could possibly live in such cold temperatures and take such big leaps across the snow. Fifty years later, herdsmen of Breuil would remember the noble stranger who had insinuated himself into their lives, the tall man who excavated the remains of a fort at the col south of the Matterhorn. Saussure believed that the Valdostans—the people living in the Aosta Valley—built the Fort de St. Théodule to defend against attacks launched by the Valaisans.

The natural scientist, geologist, and philosopher James David Forbes continued the work of Saussure. He also considered the Matterhorn to be the "most different mountain in the Alps." At that time, with alpine exploration in its infancy and mountain climbing considered an exotic pastime for wealthy people, the myth of the Matterhorn was born. The locals could not fathom why strangers, who had all possible comforts at home, came to their poor valley to hike the slopes of inhospitable and dangerous mountains, sleep in hay barns, and scale icy mountaintops when they could instead have traveled by coach through industrial cities and slept in comfortable hotels.

In the summer of 1880, around the time Napoleon and his army crossed the Great St. Bernard Pass to advance into Italy, the English crossed the Col de Saint-Théodule. They arrived in the Valais from Valtournenche, frightening the vicar of St. Niklaus, who had never had the pleasure to meet an Englishman. He hoped that the St. Niklaus Valley and his congregation would be spared the influence of tourism.

It took forty years for the village physician, Dr. Lauber, to open the first inn in the valley, the Du Mont Cervin, which had a kitchen and three guest beds. Now more and more tourists, first and foremost English, flocked to the Alps to visit this gigantic natural amphitheater. The Matterhorn, which was hailed the miracle of miracles, still only attracted the interest of scientists (Forbes was not alone in believing the "most wonderful peak in the Alps" to be unscalable).

In 1844 the English writer, painter, and philosopher John Ruskin arrived in Zermatt, where from the north he created an image of the Matterhorn that would become well known. His parents, who had taken him on a trip to the Alps when he was fourteen, had kindled his interest in the mountains, and after reading Saussure's *Voyages dans les Alpes*, given to him by his father, Ruskin found his way to nature. "Nature has given me a new life," he wrote, "which will only find its end at the gates of the mountain of no return." Through William Turner's paintings, which show mountains ravaged by thunderstorms or dipped in beautiful sunsets, the romantic philosopher learned to recognize what he called the architecture of mountains.

In 1855 Alexander Seiler, who was not a native, opened a guesthouse with six beds in Zermatt. Two years later, the English set up their exclusive Alpine Club, whose members had to prove that they had climbed higher than 13,000 feet (4,000 meters). The Matterhorn and its twenty-nine surrounding 4,000-meter peaks became their preferred playground. Interest in mountaineering was growing. English sport enthusiasts scaled more and increasingly difficult peaks with their Swiss mountain guides. Only one mountain, the Matterhorn, remained out of the question. The fact that guides believed it unscalable soon became incentive for many alpinists, however, who viewed it as a challenge.

East of the Matterhorn, a nine-year struggle for Monte Rosa ended in 1855, when its highest peak—the Dufourspitze—was conquered on August 1 by a party of eight: Matthäus and Johannes Zumtaugwald, Ulrich Lauener, Christopher and James Smyth, Charles Hudson, John Birkbeck, and Edward Stephenson. Other mountains in the Zermatt area were being scaled, and only the enigmatic Matterhorn remained untouched, as if it was taboo. "The Matterhorn can be conquered," wrote Alsatian scholar Daniel Dollfus-Ausset that year. "A balloon made of extraordinarily durable material and of a certain shape tied to a long rope . . . would allow an aeronaut to steer his gondola and land on its top."

Two years later, in 1857, three men from Breuil-Cervinia set out to explore whether their mountain, the Matterhorn, could be climbed without any tools. They mounted via the rocks of the jagged southwest ridge and reached an altitude of about 12,000 feet (3,700 meters). One of the three explorers was the legendary Jean-Antoine Carrel, born in January 1829 in Valtournenche. He came from one of three Carrel clans—poor mountain farmers from the valley at the southern base of the Matterhorn—who had been self-sufficient for generations. Married, with nine children, he lived in a small wooden cabin in Valtournenche during the winter and in nearby Avouil during the summer.

The locals divided their mountain pastures into arable and nonarable land. The mountain farmers lived semi-nomadically in places where pastures produced grass, forests produced wood, and water drove mill wheels. Hunters and poachers did not clamber higher than the chamois did, for there was nothing to be found beyond—the eternal snow was considered the limit. Neither greed nor curiosity made them want to go any farther. The locals believed that no one could possibly want to expose themselves to the dangers of those menacing glaciers and rock cliffs. They came up with the most absurd reasons to explain the huge influx of English, who surely did not come to the mountains for pure pleasure or to acquire knowledge about them. They were more likely treasure hunters, alchemists, or secret agents. Perhaps they were just fools, for only a fool goes where he is destined to die.

In the beginning, the tourists were viewed with suspicion. Jean-Antoine Carrel, however, understood their behavior and sympathized with their curiosity. Their customs were alien to him, but like everyone else in the valley he was curious. Maybe he could help them reach their goals, he thought. Most of them did not understand that mountains cannot be moved. The English alpinists had no sense of direction or any feeling for the local weather, and they failed to understand the vastness of the mountains and their dangers.

At the time, the profession of guide did not exist in Valtournenche, due to regulations and lack of equipment. The *monsieurs* arrived, and engaged porters who clambered up the surrounding mountains with them. The locals catered to every desire of the free-spending visitors.

As time passed, Carrel heard that some men had established themselves as guides on the Swiss side of the Matterhorn. The ambitious tourists trusted these guides, who were cabin owners, chamois hunters, and poachers. Climbing requires sure-footedness but also knowledge of the local phenomena, such as weather and rock structure. Once trust was established between tourist and local helper, the relationship went beyond the trip up and down the mountain. For a fee, a guide offered a service and took responsibility.

It sometimes happened that wealthy Englishmen would spend several weeks in the mountains with the same guide, Carrel noticed. He saw the main problem of these *monsieurs* as their fear of fear. They sought the help of guides since they felt insecure, and they required guides not only to carry their rucksacks but also to take ultimate responsibility. Carrel, the impoverished chamois hunter, considered himself experienced enough to take on this role, but only if he was the one who would make the decisions on the mountain.

Englishman Edward Whymper was one of these *monsieurs*. During his childhood, Whymper had never had anything to do with the Alps. His father, Josiah Wood Whymper, a successful watercolorist and engraver, lived in London with his children—nine boys and two girls. Born in 1840, Edward, the second eldest, was no prodigy.

When Edward was twelve years of age, Albert Smith launched his performance *The Ascent of Mont Blanc* in the Egyptian Hall in Piccadilly, London. The show would run for six years. With two thousand performances and eight hundred thousand visitors, the combination of diorama and lecture remains the most successful such entertainment about a mountain to this day. At the time, it spawned in England what the *Times* described as "Mont-Blanc mania." At age fourteen, Edward Whymper left school and joined his father's business, learning the trade of wood engraving. He also developed a talent for watercolor painting, which led to an opportunity to see the Alps. The publisher William Longman commissioned young Whymper to travel to the Dauphiné, as he needed some illustrations of the very rarely depicted Alps of southern France.

At age twenty, Whymper had never seen a mountain, let alone set foot upon one. Was he interested in mountaineering? No. Back then alpinism was for wealthy people. It was a new kind of sport, a sort of compensation for the upper classes during the early days of industrialization. But setting out to sketch, paint, and engrave the mountains, Whymper soon began to climb to their summits. At the end of July 1860 he visited Switzerland for the first time, and his ascent of Mont Pelvoux, a peak of almost 13,000 feet (4,000 meters) in the French Alps, was his baptism in serious climbing. At some point he heard about the unclimbed and supposedly unclimbable

Matterhorn and was hooked. He wanted to go there—he had to go there. Even though the mountain guides in Zermatt could only shake their heads about his naiveté, Whymper made this mountain his next goal.

At the time, Jean-Antoine Carrel was the only other person to believe that the Matterhorn was climbable, but he wanted to climb it from the Italian side. Conquering this mountain became a personal matter for both men. For Whymper it was an athletic challenge. For Carrel it was fueled by curiosity. Neither of the men had patriotic motives.

In the end, Carrel would not dare to climb all the way to the top with Whymper. He was not prepared to take the full responsibility for such an undertaking. Whymper would try his luck from the Swiss side without Carrel—and succeed.

The year 1865 was an important year for modern alpinism, which commenced in 1786 with the first ascent of Mont Blanc and continues to this day. More than forty first ascents between the Pyrenees and the Dolomites alone were made in the summer of 1865, including the Grandes Jorasses, Aiguille Verte, Wellenkuppe, Obergabelhorn, Auguille de Bionnassay, Breithorn, Tschingelhorn, Mont Blanc de Cheilon, Nesthorn, the Möselle, Piz Roseg, Piz Buin, Cima Tosa, Tofana di Dentro, Cevedale, and Cristallo. In addition, groundbreaking new routes were established that year, such as the Brenva Spur on the south face of Mont Blanc, the Lion Ridge on the Matterhorn, the North Pillar of the Silberhorn, and the Ortler traverse from north to south. The guiding profession was established, and mountain guide dynasties were beginning to grow in flourishing Alpine tourism towns such as Chamonix, Valtournenche, Zermatt, Grindelwald, and Cortina d'Ampezzo.

Chapter I

It is the year 1890. Carrel screams in his sleep. He lifts his head briefly, as if he has awakened.

"Did he call us?" Sinigaglia wonders.

"No," Charles Gorret, a young mountain guide, replies. "He is dreaming. Probably something about the cattle drive or hunting."

"Is he frightened?"

"What of?"

"Maybe the storm."

Gorret looks at Carrel, who is lying on the bunk, snoring. He had fallen asleep immediately after they had reached the little hut halfway up to the top of the Matterhorn.

"No. He was already asleep when the storm hit."

"Why do you think he is so terrified then?"

"Jean-Antoine is tired. He has been getting up at midnight for days: first on Mont Blanc and then for the traverse across the passes from Chamonix to Courmayeur."

"I understand. He must be exhausted."

"Shall we go down?" Sinigaglia asks, rubbing his hands over the fire.

Gorret shakes his head, inspects the Italian from the side, and murmurs something like: "No, no." No, they will certainly not go back. Gorret needs the money to support his young family. The Matterhorn is his workplace.

Fire crackles in the small brick stove; the storm rattles the roof.

As he is waking up, Carrel looks around, sniffs at the air in the smoke-filled room, and listens to the storm, like a startled animal.

"What's happening with the storm?" he asks, still sleepy.

"It came quickly, just out of the blue," says Gorret.

"I don't like it." A long silence follows. "Is there any fresh snow?"

"Hail and snow."

"How much?"

"I don't know."

Still trying to wake up, Carrel realizes that an ascent of the Matterhorn is out of the question. Descending is also going to be extremely difficult as the rocks are hidden under the snow and glazed with ice. His route is in pretty poor condition. But what worries him most is the thought of being stuck here for days. Should they risk a descent anyway? Right now? Hunkering down inside the hut for the duration of the storm could turn into a nightmare.

Sinigaglia is keen to wait, though, at least for another night.

Then the two mountain guides agree on a plan.

"As soon as the wind eases, we are going down," says Carrel. "Tomorrow. It's too late today."

"When tomorrow?" Sinigaglia wants to know.

"With the first daylight."

"All three of us?"

"Of course. Sinigaglia, you as the guest must always be in the middle."

"Can we not postpone the descent?" Sinigaglia is still hoping for better weather—after all, he is the paying client.

"The wind is too strong," Carrel replies. "I guess it will take weeks for the conditions to improve and make a summit attempt possible."

"Why?"

The wind has carried the snow everywhere: it is stuck in the cracks, on the ridges, on the rock bands. Carrel lifts his blanket, sits up with a groan, and lumbers down from his bunk. He does not look sleepy; he looks old. His face is gaunt, his back slightly bent, his beard ashen. Only his eyes, wide open now, show life and sparkle. He puts on his boots—hobnailed ankle-high leather boots usually worn by farmers, who work in the woods high up on the mountain—and walks toward the door. The floor creaks even though he floats across it like a seasick ghost, as if he wants to scare away the storm outside.

When he first steps outside, he does not see a thing. But once his eyes get used to the darkness, he can detect swirling snowflakes. The storm tugs on his tweed jacket; the wet cold air forces its way down his lungs. The steps leading from the platform to the ascent trail have completely disappeared under the fresh snow. Then he looks up. The overhanging rock on the big tower directly above the hut seems even more terrifying than the abyss below. And where did the rest of the world go? Carrel glimpses the winter moon hiding behind the racing clouds far away in the distance, and it seems like he's on another planet.

"The skies have gone," Gorret hears the old man say when he steps back into the hut. Carrel shakes off the snow, lifts his head, and murmurs something. Even Sinigaglia has now come to terms with it: it does not look good.

When they had reached the hut late in the morning, they had come across Daniele, Antonio, and Pierre Maquignaz and Edoardo Bich, who had fixed some rope higher up on the mountain. These young mountain guides had bolstered Sinigaglia's hope that the following day would be glorious: Carrel would be able to lead his team safely to the summit. At around three o'clock in the afternoon, the Maquignaz group had descended to Breuil. Carrel's gaze had followed the four after he'd bid them goodbye with a wave. Then he had wanted to take a short nap.

Now back in the hut, Carrel remains silent.

He checks the weather one more time. Storm clouds have moved in from Mont Blanc, obscuring the sky and turning it into a turbulent ocean. When he steps out of the hut for the third time, the storm has already reached the Dent d'Hérens; the seracs and delicate ice ridges over there have disappeared, and the big mountain in the west seems to have descended into chaos: like an expressionist painting in blue and black.

Carrel hopes that it is only a passing thunderstorm, but deep down he suspects trouble and feels uneasy. The northerly winds are getting stronger by the hour. Carrel reviews the situation and relives the worst weather conditions in his time as a mountain guide, as if he had to draw survival powers from life-threatening situations of the past. He is responsible; he must not make a mistake and worry his client. Had they carried on to the summit—as his client had wanted to do—they would be sitting on the other side now, on the descent, trapped. They would be stranded somewhere high up on the mountain without protection.

Even Sinigaglia has finally accepted that they would probably be dead if Carrel had not insisted that they wait and see. Had the old man predicted this sudden change in the weather? Did he suspect what was coming? The weather has only turned worse since the four young mountain guides left the hut, and neither Sinigaglia nor Gorret have ever before experienced such a quick drop in temperature. What a storm! First they were hit by sudden snowfall, then sleet.

"You should have woken me up," Carrel says to Gorret. It is not meant as a reproach but could be a warning for the future.

It is too late to follow the young men down to the valley. In the evening the wind suddenly changes direction. Shortly afterward, a hailstorm descends on the Matterhorn so violently that it chills Carrel to the bone. The incessant rumbling of thunder and rockfall seems endless, as if their mountain were breaking down below and above them. Bolts of lightning flash through the pitch-black night, and the electrically charged air shimmers. For two hours it seems as if the Northern Lights are knocking on the small windows of the hut. Again and again, the lightning illuminates the interior of the hut, as bright as daylight. The storm lasts the whole night and continues for another day and another night.

Despite being wrapped up in blankets, Carrel is shivering. He feels helpless and in his dreams sees himself fading away. As if all his experience was worthless, his energy depleted, and his courage nothing but the hubris of a madman.

Outside snow continues to fall, and the wind continues to rattle the roof and walls of the hut. The temperature has dropped to far below freezing, and the window facing downslope is covered with snow. The temperature inside the hut has also dropped to below zero, covering everything with a sheet of ice. "It would be impossible to survive outside," Carrel says. Fortunately, the hut is well-built. Is it not named after him? Did he not help construct it? What would have happened if the hut had never been built? He does not even want to entertain the idea.

"A hasty descent would mean certain death," Carrel says quietly.

When they have run out of firewood and other provisions, Carrel considers descending despite the danger, despite zero visibility. The large amount of fresh snow worries him most. His sixth sense instructs him to wait a bit longer. So they wrap themselves in blankets, burn the furniture—benches, a loose shelf, a table—and wait. The fear of freezing to death becomes unbearable. In a daydream, Carrel sees himself descending to the valley (he has done it hundreds of times), and all the hardship people have suffered on his mountain spring to his mind. His head is spinning with an infinite loop of images. Like so many times before, he has to make it down to the valley with a client. He has to bring all three of them back alive. For this he bears the sole responsibility.

CHAPTER 2

IN TWILIGHT OF A SUMMER evening in 1857, three men stand in front of a squalid-looking hut in Avouil, where the narrow valley starts to widen, offering magnificent views across alpine pastures all the way up to the glaciers. The men converse using sign language since a roaring glacial stream makes it impossible to hear. They look as if they want to conjure the mountain, which sparkles like a crystal against the setting sun. From nowhere else in the valley does the Matterhorn look so determined: a blunt, giant wedge reaching high into the sky.

"Tomorrow morning, then," one of the men says, just as he is setting off.

"Good night," the second one says.

"See you tomorrow."

"At the crack of dawn," the third man emphasizes.

The three men arrange to approach their meeting point from different directions, taking exactly the same routes they are taking now to return to their homes.

Avouil, a conglomeration of small farms at the lower edge of the southern slopes, is home to a handful of families in the summer. From here, the herders drive their cattle to the upper slopes. Here they store butter, cheese, and firewood.

Before dawn, when the stars are just beginning to vanish from the sky, the three men tread toward the mountain. People in Avouil are under the impression that the trio is setting out to catch marmots. They take along a "grafio"—a long ash-wood rod topped with an iron hook that is used for marmot hunting.

On this clear morning, the three odd-looking figures head toward the Matterhorn, which the elders in the valley call La Gran Becca—the Big Beak. Jean-Jacques Carrel, a relative of Jean-Antoine, is one of them. Clad in dark clothes, gaunt, with a wide-brimmed hat on his head, he is the most senior and seems to be the leader. He is a hunter with a formidable knowledge of the territory and a sensitivity that sometimes comes close to that of a wild animal. When looking for mountain goats on the steep southern slopes of the Matterhorn, he runs, climbs, and jumps as if he were a mountain goat himself. With his weather-beaten face, wrinkled hands, and slanted eyes that are usually hidden beneath the broad brim of his hat, he is a singular character in the valley. The time he has spent hunting game in adverse weather, loitering on mountain pastures and in rocky ravines high up on the mountain has left its mark. He is extremely self-confident but not too proud. Like all men of the valley, he does not talk much, goes to church on Sundays, and works hard during the week. Almost a quarter of a century ago he proved his extraordinary courage by being the only man who dared to climb down a crevasse on the Theodul Glacier to rescue an injured person. And this willingness to risk his life is still within him.

The second in the group is Jean-Antoine Carrel, who looks like an outlaw. His fierce demeanor and fearlessness have made him an outsider in the valley, where the locals mockingly call him the Cock of Valtournenche. Amé Gorret, the third in the group, is much younger than the other two. An aspiring priest, he may be curious, but he is certainly more prudent than the others.

With Jean-Jacques in the lead, the three men continue toward the mountain. After a few winters of secret discussions and lonely summers on the mountain pastures, where they have spent more and more time gazing at the Matterhorn, they now want to find out how high their mountain will allow them to go. They are sure-footed and have stamina—excellent walkers. Moving in sync and without saying a single word, they go about their business, which looks somewhat illicit.

At the Weiler Planet pasture, they come upon herders Gabriel Maquignaz and Victor Carrel. (Victor is known as "the painter"). They chat about marmots and the weather, but nobody says a word about their real intentions. When the three "hunters" continue, the herders bid them goodbye and shake their heads as if they do not want to be accomplices in such a dangerous and clandestine high-altitude hunt.

A little higher up, the trio comes across a shepherd, who greets them with a wave. They respond by swinging their grafios in the air and then accelerate their ascent.

"A bad day for the marmots," they hear the shepherd say as they pass his herd. Soon they are so far in the distance that to the shepherd they are reduced to three black dots on the steep slope.

At the highest pasture, they are finally out of sight of other humans. The grazing cows fixing their large eyes upon them and curious goats sniffling the salt on their clothes are the only creatures they encounter up here.

The men stop and listen. All they can hear is the whistling of marmots, the flapping wings of an eagle circling around the isolated white fluffy clouds, and the meltwater roaring in the glacier above them. They can take their time now. When they slowly approach the tree line, they see marmots everywhere scurry into their holes.

Once they reach the moraine of the Matterhorn Glacier, they turn to the rocky ridge to the left of the glacier. "Keu de Tzarciglion," says Jean-Jacques, who knows every single rock and could probably name them. His grandfather has been up here hunting for mountain chamois.

For a few hours, they clamber up along the ridge without a definite plan, without uttering a word. Everything goes smoothly; only the sight of the jagged rocky cliffs farther along to the right looks menacing. Just before they reach the highest point of the saddle left of the Matterhorn, they part. Jean-Jacques makes his way across the hard snow, while the other two stay on the rock, which seems to them to be a safer ascent route. Suddenly, Gorret hears a cry for help. Jean-Jacques is unable to move forward or backward. He is stuck and one wrong move could throw him off balance and send him rolling down hundreds of feet into the abyss. The ice is so steep and slippery in this place that arresting a fall would be impossible.

Jean-Antoine is the first to come out of his brief shock-induced paralysis. He is the most accomplished climber of all three men and takes command. The "Bersagliere," as Jean-Antoine is known in the valley due to his past in the army, and Amé Gorret, the priest, hurry to help. With their canes firmly in one hand, they hold onto each other and carefully inch their way across the ice. When they finally reach the hunter, Jean-Antoine takes out an ax and cuts steps into the ice to allow all three of them to return safely to the rocks.

"You should only climb a mountain with your equals," Jean-Antoine thinks. He does not say it out loud, but he will never forget this epiphany, and it will apply to all his future climbing expeditions.

Out of breath, the three gain the crest of the ridge between the Tête du Lion and the Dent d'Hérens from where they can see the Swiss side of the mountain range for the first time. A completely new world opens up to them. Almost terrified, they gaze down toward the Tiefenmatten Glacier spreading out 1,600 feet (500 meters) beneath them. Have they not been told that the village of Hérens lay behind the Matterhorn? For centuries, the people of Valtournenche have believed that there was civilization beyond the mountains. But there is no village, only a valley completely covered in ice and enclosed by enormous rocks offering an overwhelming view into the abyss. For a few moments the three men remain silent, staggered by the stillness of this new world, which is completely different from their lush native valley and the paradise the vicar preaches about from his pulpit. They are stupefied by the sheer drops and jagged glaciers surrounded by soaring peaks, which are not significant enough for the farmers of Breuil to name them. They stand on the saddle separating their native valley from the wilderness beyond. On their left the ridge leads to the summit of the Dent d'Hérens; on their right the Tête du Lion rises up toward the Matterhorn.

Suddenly one of the three men starts pushing rocks over the cliff into the abyss. They follow the course of the heavy rocks and are fascinated by the way they whirl up clouds of powdery snow on their fast descent before they crash against the rock wall farther down and disappear completely in the huge throat of the glacier below.

They are in no hurry. They are tired, but the sun is high in the sky and the Matterhorn seems near at hand. From here the mountain's rocky gorges look more defined than from Avouil. And the summit towers high above them! Jean-Antoine is convinced that he will reach it one day.

"Strange," says one of them. "From this perspective the Matterhorn appears less daunting than from the valley."

Even though the mountain does not belong to them—or maybe it does, since nobody can carry it away—Jean-Antoine makes the Matterhorn his goal on this very day.

The two other men have given up their intentions of reaching the summit but continue climbing out of pure curiosity. They find no difficulty in reaching the Tête du Lion, from where they see the big chasm separating them from the real Matterhorn for the first time. On the other side, which still seems unreachable, the steep summit rock reaches high into the sky.

On their descent along the southern flank of the Tête du Lion, they discover a row of climbable rocky ledges leading to the base of the Matterhorn, which seems much easier than their ascent route so far.

CHAPTER 3

IN VALTOURNENCHE, LOCALS HAVE STARTED to realize Jean-Antoine's obsession with the Matterhorn, which they also call the "devil's mountain." Its flanks, they say, are the gates to hell, and its peak is for ghosts only. "It's certainly not made for humans," the vicar says.

Jean-Antoine Carrel does not respond to these comments. He is convinced that the Matterhorn can be scaled. When Carrel's uncle Kanonikus, a vicar from Aosta, who rarely comes to Valtournenche these days, finds out about Jean-Antoine's climb, he plays it down: the excursion, he says, is nothing but an imprudent escapade and is not even worth talking about. But deep down inside he also believes in the possibility of climbing the Matterhorn. He admires his nephew's skills, courage, and energy. He has been thinking about exploring the mountains surrounding Aosta for a long time. Back in the days when nobody in the valley had yet thought of studying the Alps, Kanonikus had been shrewd enough to build an observatory on the roof of his vicarage. It would become one of the most important meteorological research stations in Italy. He had been keeping records, collecting data about plants, weather, and glaciers. Following his passion has meant a constant fight against the prejudice of his compatriots, who think his yearning for science and climbing peaks is nothing but foolhardy and useless.

Kanonikus has known the Matterhorn since his youth. When he climbs high enough he can see it towering above all other lesser hills surrounding Aosta and he marvels: "La Gran Becca! Even if it cannot claim the glory of being the highest peak in Europe, it is undeniably the most beautiful!" For decades he has been preoccupied with the question of whether the mountain is climbable and whether it would be responsible to do so. Are humans allowed to take risks that are not entirely controllable? Even if the purpose is of no use whatsoever?

He calls it "my Matterhorn," cherishing the hope that he himself will scramble up its slopes one day and be solely responsible for it. For him, climbing this mountain is almost a sacrament. But isn't every hike an act of purification, every ascent a pilgrimage? An added value is that his native valley would certainly become famous once tourists know that the Matterhorn is climbable. He is also aware that it would increase the wealth of the valley. Regardless, the mighty rocky pyramid is priceless.

It is now 1857, and Jean-Antoine is climbing with his brother and Amé Gorret. Does the vicar know that Gabriel Maquignaz and Victor Carrel are at the same time exploring another ascent route up the mountain? They climb the east face of the Tête du Lion but are nearly killed by tumbling rocks. They return to their mountain pastures shocked and taciturn.

Chapter 4

In 1861, twenty-one-year-old Edward Whymper aspires to make the first ascents of two summits in the Alps, the Weisshorn and the Matterhorn. With only two Alpine summers under his belt, the youngster reaches for the stars, having chosen the most difficult 13,000-foot (4,000-meter) peaks. He is driven, certainly, and powered by the hubris of youth. Upon his arrival in Breuil, he learns that Irish-born physicist John Tyndall, one of the most successful alpinists of the time, has already conquered the Weisshorn. While most still consider the Matterhorn unscalable, Tyndall too has come to Breuil and like Whymper hopes to achieve the first ascent. The professor has gained a good reputation in Valtournenche and is known to be generous toward his guides and amiable toward his porters. Not so with Whymper. The villagers think he goes around on foot because he can't afford a horse-drawn carriage, but Whymper is not destitute, he is parsimonious. He has also not been favorably impressed by his experience with guides. To him they are porters and pathfinders, great consumers of meat and drink, but little more. He would much prefer the company of his countrymen to those he sees as primitive hunters or herders, those locals who call themselves guides. In his view, these alpine peasants lack nobility. To him, their faces express malice, their gestures show arrogance, and their demands seem greedy. On top of that, he thinks they are envious of his wealth, that they are xenophobic and devious.

Despite his misgivings about the locals, Whymper embarks on a search for the best possible companion to climb the Matterhorn. All unanimously declare Jean-Antoine Carrel to be the man for him.

In a dingy smoke-filled hut in Avouil, a cabin with tiny windows and a door requiring him to duck, Whymper finds a middle-aged man. The man seems to come from a proletarian background but is obviously a clever fellow. His face—marked by piercing eyes, a hooked nose, and a beard—seems dismissive and inviting at the same time.

"Are you Carrel?" Whymper asks.

"Yes. Jean-Antoine."

"My name is Whymper, and I am looking for a guide to climb the Matterhorn."

"Are you alone?"

"No, I'm with an Englishman and a Swiss mountain guide."

"The Matterhorn is very difficult."

"I know, but this is exactly why I am here. I need the best man in the valley."

"Wait a minute. What other mountains have you climbed?"

"Many. Last year I studied the Matterhorn when I walked from Zermatt to Breuil."

Carrel listens and thinks.

"How much?" he asks Whymper.

"Twenty francs a day, whatever the result."

Carrel agrees but demands to take a second man, a comrade of his, for safety reasons. Whymper, who shies away from expenses, declines.

"I already have a guide."

"Two guides for two clients is not enough."

"No, it is enough. I climb independently."

"I insist that my comrade come," Carrel says.

"Why?"

"The responsibility lies with us."

"I am responsible for myself. So why should we hire your man?"

"We need him!"

"Is the route that difficult?"

"Long and very difficult. Maybe too difficult for a foreigner in white trousers," Carrel adds, speaking in his local dialect, which he supposes Whymper does not understand.

"Why too difficult for us English?"

"You don't know the mountain."

"I only need one local man to show me the way."

"I'll only come if I can bring one of my men."

"Why are you so stubborn?"

"Either hire one of our guides, or I am not coming."

"Why do we need so many people?"

"In case we have to retreat, for instance."

"I count on being successful."

"Even if we reach the summit, we will all have to come back alive somehow."

"Of course. But more people pose more risks, require more effort and more time."

"Yes, of course."

"So, why do we need a second man? You are a guide, aren't you?"

"It is impossible without a second man."

"How do you know?"

"The Matterhorn is not like Mont Blanc or Monte Rosa. All attempts to scale this mountain have failed—from Breuil as well as from Zermatt."

"So?"

"Half a dozen attempts, in vain."

"I can make it, all the same!"

"Maybe to your grave," Carrel warns.

"Ah, you are scared. That's why you want a second guide."

Whymper is in his element. He wants Carrel to join his expedition and tries to convince him using humiliation.

"Not only scared," Carrel says calmly.

"So, what else?"

"If things go wrong, how would I get you down the mountain on my own?"

"Don't worry. I will certainly be able to get myself down, and I can assure you that I climb at least as well as the peasants in this valley."

"Still, I don't want to be responsible for your heroic act."

Jean-Antoine Carrel is determined. With his right hand he knocks on the paneled wall of the room. A male voice replies from the other side, and then a heavily built bearded figure with long dangling arms appears out of the darkness. It is Carrel's comrade. Whymper, terrified, gives a condescending gesture and walks toward the door. The negotiations are broken off.

CHAPTER 5

EVEN WHEN DEFIANT, EDWARD WHYMPER looks good. He strides back to Breuil, clad in brightly colored pants, his shoulder bag swung over his right shoulder, a small fashionable hat on his head. The whole way he has a clear view of the Matterhorn. "What on earth am I doing here in this depressing place with its simple peasants?" he asks himself. He would certainly not be here if it were not for the Matterhorn, the most remarkable mountain he has ever set eyes on. The mere thought of surmounting those huge glaciers and vertical rock cliffs beyond the gloomy woods makes him feel as if he is planning a prison escape. He pictures himself reaching that last virgin alpine summit, the one of such captivating individuality, the one that rises proudly above all. But down here in the village live these unkempt peasants he is dependent on and who make him wait.

It is not arrogance that nurtures his pride, it is the mountain—his mountain. Whymper is convinced: the first ascent will be as unique as the summit itself. Carrel's demand outrages him. If need be, he will tackle the Matterhorn alone.

"I am perfectly capable of doing what these peasants do," he thinks.

People step aside when they come across him on the small path leading to the village. Some nearing him disappear into huts. Are they avoiding him? These alpine farmers' clothes are plain, heavily worn, and often patched. Their faces seem sinister to Whymper, their expressions serious, without a trace of a smile. Even the little houses—dark huts lined up closely together—have an uninviting, dreary air about them. As if they were built as a defense against hopelessness, as if they had to take turns protecting each other from the cold, as if they had joined forces to resist thunderstorms and high winds. Life here is hard, and the villagers suffer silently. They live in constant fear of their animals starving, of avalanches thundering down, their houses collapsing under the heavy snow. Summers are short, and winters dominate the valley for most of the year. During the cold months, the alpine farmer sits patiently by the fire, sleeps in his dingy hut, and waits and waits and waits. Or he prays. He prays for the sun to return. Spring passes very quickly. Harvest time is arduous, and the first autumn snow plunges the village back into deep resignation. This is how it goes, over and over again.

Having passed the shabby huts, Whymper can now see the church steeple, with its bells that convey the same sad sound to the people every day. The bells announce births and funerals, accidents and weddings. Even religion seems to stir fear in this remote place. The paintings on the church walls do not imply hope and love, but rather martyrdom and death.

This world is alien to Whymper, and disconcerting. He is an artist from London. He does not pity the people here; he despises them. This is why he cannot get over Carrel's rejection of his offer, his insistence on Whymper hiring an additional man. Is he not hungry for money? Does he think that all English are rich good-for-nothings or snobs?

The dull misery of the people of the valley, who live amid the most magnificent mountain scenery, makes Whymper feel out of place. Nature to them means nothing but the fight for survival, he thinks. What relationship do they have with the Matterhorn? None whatsoever!

"Let them starve without my money," he grumbles to himself when he reaches the first houses in Breuil. "Let them stay down here forever!"

CHAPTER 6

CARREL AND HIS PEOPLE ARE content with what earth can provide them at such high altitudes. They have no extravagant yearnings. They have resigned themselves to living within the narrow-minded valley society and do not allow themselves to have exotic dreams. As everyone in the valley does similar work, there is no feeling of shame but rather a feeling of equality and justice.

The locals are self-sufficient. They barter their products, as money is a rare commodity. Only frugality can flourish, given such poor soil. A family's security relies on a small piece of land and a hut. There one is born, and there one will die, under the sky whose infinity is limited only by the lines of mountain ranges.

The Swiss scientist Saussure, who played an essential role in the first ascent of Mont Blanc by offering a financial incentive, arrived in this poverty-stricken world by mule. He did not come as a conqueror; he came as a researcher. And he came twice. Five years after having scaled the highest mountain in the Alps—it was the third ascent—he dedicated his time to the most beautiful peak, the Matterhorn. On his first visit, the people of Valtournenche did not know anything about him or his motives. But once they realized what they could gain from such a visitor, the cattle breeders, farmers, hunters, and smugglers hoped that others would follow this generous researcher and that tourism would bring wealth to the people. Especially the women, the mothers, wished for some extra income, as it was their duty to manage the money, provide the meals, sew the clothes, do the laundry, and bring up the children. In some times of bad harvest, provisions were barely enough to get through the winter.

For the time being, everything remains the same. Twice a year, every family in the valley goes through an almost sacred ritual, baking their traditional rye bread, sometimes over the course of several days and nights. The bread has to last until the end of the winter, and after six months it is so hard that the village elders can only consume it when it's softened in milk. As for the men, on the most beautiful winter days they clamber up above the valley to collect wood they stacked up during summer, load it on their sledges, and bring it down. In between these periodic outings, they sit and wait.

In mid-June, many of the valley dwellers move up to the alpine pastures where they look after their own cattle or work as herdsmen or shepherds on common pastures. In the course of the season, both cattle and men slowly go higher as they move from pasture to pasture. Once the cattle have consumed the grass of one meadow, they go farther up until eventually they reach the highest meadow, where grass only grows in a few spots and where the slopes are almost too steep for the animals. They advance all the way to the moraine at the base of the Matterhorn. The herders often take their youngest children, who either become very strong at this altitude or too sick to survive. But in time for Michaelmas, the September 29 feast of Saint Michael the Archangel, everyone goes back down to the valley.

Once again they sit in their front rooms, the windows covered with straw, a small oil lamp often their only source of light, and they tell stories. The fathers pass on the tales just as they heard them from the village elders. They recount century-old myths of unknown origin and talk about Pagan-Christian traditions. They talk about souls rising from purgatory, aimlessly wandering across the mountain slopes in their quest to find peace; about dwarves emerging from sparkling caves in the light of the winter moon; about the gold and jewels that make the summit of La Gran Becca glitter in the last sunlight of the day. The myth of treasures hidden in the bosom of the mountain has long fired the imagination of the poor mountain folk, and a few herders have brought down lumps of crystal from high up as evidence. The sparkle has existed since before the time of the mountaineers. In secret places in the Alps one can still see scrape marks, hundreds of years old.

Far up, where La Gran Becca reaches high into the sky, thunderstorms and dark clouds gather like smoke rising from hell. The locals have observed strange figures surfacing from the mist, and many of them are convinced that the devil lives up there. It is Satan who unceasingly hurls rocks down into the valley, makes avalanches thunder, and creates lightning.

But herdsmen up in the highest hut, which is named after the wind god Eurus and is nestled right at the foot of La Gran Becca, recount the tale of Théodule, a bishop from Sitten, in the Valais, who came to Valtournenche from the other side of the mountain in the fourth century AD. He accessed the valley via the col that was later named after him. He did not make this journey to do wonders but rather to visit the hermits Evantius and Juvenal. At that time, a small child was bitten by a venomous snake in Breuil, and nobody was able to help. Théodule, who was already a bishop but not yet a saint, simply murmured a prayer and saved the child's life.

After this curious visit, more and more people crossed the col from the Valais, the fertile valley in the north. They came to trade, barter animals, or visit relatives. A few worshippers went to Aosta as pilgrims. The pass, which used to be called Col du Mont Cervin—or simply Mont Cervin—had more significance than the Matterhorn, which was merely considered a landmark. The name "Mont Cervin"—just as the names "Matterberg" or "Mattenberg"— originally referred to the Col de Saint-Théodule or to the whole area south of the Matterhorn. Long before it was called the Matterhorn, every village community gave the mountain its own name, depending on what it looked like from their perspective. Legend has it that pilgrims used to travel to Switzerland as part of a procession from Valtournenche. They came from Breuil, reached the chapel at the Schwarzsee (Black Lake) via the col, and continued to Sitten. Faith was much stronger than curiosity. The mountain above the col was taboo.

Between 1746 and 1861, six of the members of the Gorret family were priests. The parents of Amé Gorret, the man who took part in the first attempt to climb the Matterhorn, chose a spiritual life for him from a very early age. They trusted their son to the care of a vicar, and under his supervision Amé continued his studies. The vicar was strict, but he encouraged Amé to go mountain climbing, not only because Amé was being educated to become a priest to mountain dwellers but also because the mountains were considered proof of God's existence.

Despite the Enlightenment, a strong conservative spirit was still alive in the Aosta Valley in the years before mountaineering. The Valdostans were adamant about keeping their parents' language, their traditions, and their religious holidays. And they remained Italian patriots. They had the pride of an insular people and wanted to keep the uniqueness of their existence. At the time, when there were no guides or inns in the valley south of the Matterhorn, most travelers passed the night in the vicarage called "The Cure," maybe because the priest of Valtournenche and the cleric of the Aosta Valley were close friends.

It is not until the arrival of the Swiss, French, and English travelers of the nineteenth century, people who belong to the most progressive and richest urban class, that the horizon of the local people widens. The tourists leave behind the meticulous order of their northern towns and venture to the mountains, where they find neither roads nor safety measures. Flocking from afar, they arrive in villages where modest alpine farmers live in medieval simplicity. A shock for both sides! Edward Whymper, who embarked on his first journey from Biona in the Valpelline to Breuil on August 28, 1860, cannot believe how backward these people seem, how dirty, how unhygienic their practices. He cannot get over it, calls them cretins, and describes their life as an impossibility. Nevertheless, he returns the following year.

CHAPTER 7

"HOW ARROGANT!" JEAN-ANTOINE CARREL SAYS angrily when Favre, the proprietor of the modest and recently opened Hotel Monte Rosa, shows him an entry in the visitors' book. "Edward Whymper en route for the Matterhorn," it says in English. The entry is dated August 27, 1861. Whymper's neat handwriting is easy to read.

"He is young," Favre says in defense of his guest.

"Too young and too arrogant. He's a dandy and not a mountaineer."

"He is obsessed with the Matterhorn."

"He doesn't even know the mountain."

"Still, he dares an ascent."

"And I'll have to bring him down if things go wrong."

"He won't get very far."

"Still, a rescue up there is impossible."

"He may not even find the start of the climb," Favre muses.

"Of course he will."

"Jean-Antoine, you're the only one who knows the way to the summit."

"Even though the herders up there fear the mountain like the devil, they'll help him find the route."

"Why?"

"He'll probably tempt them by offering money or appealing to their local pride."

"You mean because they consider the Matterhorn to be the highest mountain in the Alps, even in the world?"

"Our valley dwellers don't know anything. They don't know anything about the mountain or about the world," Carrel says.

"But Whymper knows that there are no witches or ghosts to be found up there."

"Still, no city dweller will ever get there if we don't prepare the way. Thunderstorms, rockfall, disorientation, ice and snow—these are all constant companions up there. The vertical cliffs are ten times higher than our church tower."

"Does this frighten you?"

"It frightens everyone."

"And this Whymper fellow still wants to go up?"

"Apparently. He seems fearless."

"Jean-Antoine, did you not mention an invisible fence foreigners are not allowed to climb over?"

"This obviously doesn't pose an obstacle to him."

"And the difficulties start beyond the fence?"

"Yes. And so does full responsibility."

That evening Favre tells his English guest about this conversation: "Carrel has built a fence around the Matterhorn."

"How high?"

"I don't know."

"What is the fence for?"

"Foreigners."

"So we can't go any higher?" Whymper inquires.

"Not without his blessing."

"Ridiculous."

"It's also in the interest of spirituality."

Whymper can only snigger.

The next morning, locals point to the towers and cliffs that can be seen high up on the mountain with the naked eye.

"That is the devil's abode, not that of the gods," they say.

"Superstitions," Whymper replies.

As if they did not understand his French, the farmers stare at him, mouths agape.

"Cretins," the Englishman thinks.

"Crazy," the farmers whisper to each other. The devil himself will hurl rocks at him! They say that the Parker brothers attempted the summit twice from Zermatt, and twice they failed. Nobody was surprised at this.

Their side of the mountain, the flank visible from Breuil, consists of rocky towers lined with cracks and steep rock bands with snowy patches. The ridges are cracked by frost, the gorges washed out by glacial waters, and the summit looks like the back of an eagle's head. The Beak can only be recognized as such from the other side.

The Matterhorn is never silent but gives off constant sounds of falling rocks, gusts howling around the ridges, thundering avalanches, and water-falls. As if the rock masses were alive, this monstrous mountain never stops moving.

There is only one person who can read the mountain's surface, and that is Jean-Antoine Carrel. He does not talk about it, but he has identified an ascent route on the Italian side of the mountain, hidden in the maze of rock that towers above Breuil like a sphinx. Did the English not have to give up right at the base on the other side of the mountain?

Seen from Zermatt on the northeast side, the mountain appears narrow. From Zermatt the Matterhorn almost seems to be hovering above the range. Its ridges and cliffs appear steeper there and immensely high. You have to crane your neck way back to see the summit. But if you climb from Val-tournenche to Breuil, the mountain is always in your sight as it stands tall above a wide valley floor. From here, the southwest, the Matterhorn sits on a broad foundation, immovable, made of pyramids stacked on top of each other. From this perspective, the mountain actually seems scalable.

Whymper knows of every single attempt from Breuil but wonders why the ascent is deemed easier from this jagged side of the mountain. He has only returned to Valtournenche because the Zermatt guides have refused to climb the mountain from their side. He hears rumors about hunters who repeatedly go up in different groups. How high have they reached? Up to a point that Whymper pinpoints at about 12,600 feet (3,850 meters) above the valley floor. When guides tell him that Professor Tyndall has failed in his attempt, Whymper feels no schadenfreude. He just feels satisfaction to be living in the right era.

Whymper knows that, as early as 1859, the Englishman Vaughan Hawkins was convinced that the Matterhorn could be conquered from Breuil. Hawkins's guide Johann Joseph Bennen was of the opinion that the southwest ridge would lead to the summit. A year later, Bennen engaged Jean-Jacques Carrel as a porter during the first attempts. Hawkins, Tyndall, Bennen, and Carrel aimed for the gully between the little and great peaks, and, in August 1860, they had managed to climb the rocks abutting against the Couloir du Lion on its south side to attain the Col du Lion. Once on the Matterhorn's southwest ridge, they succeeded in negotiating the first steep step but were soon forced to stop. Tyndall urged that they continue higher, but Hawkins gave up and Carrel stayed with him. Someone needed to attend to the foreigner. When Tyndall and Bennen could not advance any higher, they also turned back. They were running out of time and had to descend before darkness. Whymper asked if there were any earlier attempts that reached higher. Carrel did not reply.

Whymper will have to scale his mountain soon if he wants to be the first. Tyndall is in Breuil but has not achieved anything of significance. Whymper intends to sleep as high as possible on the mountain and reach the summit the following day. After Jean-Antoine Carrel's rejection, he endeavors to engage someone else to accompany him but without success. Matthias zum Taugwald and some other well-known Valais guides refuse to have anything to do with the Matterhorn. But there is one guide Whymper has not yet approached: Peter Taugwalder, a sturdy mountain guide from Zermatt, a man in the prime of his life.

"Two hundred francs per day, no matter whether we make it to the top or not," Taugwalder demands.

"That much?" Whymper is appalled. He realizes that Taugwalder's impossibly high price is not due to aversion toward him, but to fear of the Matterhorn.

"For every attempt?" Whymper wants to know.

"The same."

"This is ten times as much as Carrel asked for."

"Has Carrel not refused?"

"Yes, but it wasn't because of the money."

Whymper's budget is tight. Carrel may have only asked for a tenth of Taugwalder's fee, but there were questions about who would be ultimately responsible.

"Guides who only accompany me for the money will take the first opportunity to turn back," Whymper thinks, and breaks off the negotiations. Now he is absolutely sure. Only one man knows where and how to conquer the mountain: Jean-Antoine Carrel.

Chapter 8

THE FOLLOWING DAY, WHYMPER AND his Chamonix guide set out for the mountain. They pass the night in the highest cow shed, where the cow herders do their best to make the Englishman as comfortable as possible. Foreigners and herders are sitting around the great copper pot hanging over the fire when the door opens and Jean-Antoine and Jean-Jacques Carrel appear from the darkness.

"Oh, ho," Whymper thinks. "Carrel has repented."

"Not at all," says Carrel, who seems to be able to read the Englishman's thoughts. "You deceive yourself."

"Then why have you come here?"

"Because we are going on the mountain tomorrow ourselves."

"Then it's not necessary to have more than two people after all?"

"Not for us."

"You mean it's impossible for us Englishmen."

"Exactly," Carrel responds.

"So you are saying that you don't trust my abilities," Whymper responds.

"We only know how big and dangerous this mountain is."

Deep down Whymper admires Carrel for his pluck, his shrewdness, and especially for his pride. He has a strong inclination to engage the pair despite what has transpired. Whymper has come to realize that Jean-Antoine is not a simple alpine yokel. He had been a soldier and was a member of an elite corps with high distinctions, the Bersaglieri riflemen. And he is the only one who, like himself, believes it possible to scale the Matterhorn. "A man without comparison, the best mountaineer of his time. He is the only man who persistently refuses to accept defeat and continues to believe in spite of all discouragements that the great mountain is not inaccessible and that it can be ascended from the side of his native valley," Whymper writes in his travel log.

Just before dawn, both Carrels rise out of the hay, drink a bit of milk, and bid goodbye to the herdsmen. Noiselessly they disappear into the darkness. Whymper does not leave until nearly seven in the morning. He seems in no hurry, practically sauntering, following his French guide across the gentian-studded slopes toward the Glacier du Lion before they continue across the right bank of the glacier. They scramble across old hard beds of snow. Via a long natural staircase, which they name the Great Staircase and which Carrel had identified as the best route to the summit a few years earlier, they eventually reach the Col du Lion, where they pass the night.

In the morning, thick fog rises up from the gorge of the Tiefenmatten Glacier. It billows higher and higher, embracing the mountain, and in the end leaves only a few holes that reveal vertical wilderness high above and the glacier embedded between rock and ice far below. That is all they can see. It appears as if the world is boiling in a huge kettle below them. Everything is gloomy, mysterious, and menacing at the same time. Whymper refuses to admit it, but looking into the abyss gives him a fright. A stone he hurls down toward the Tiefenmatten Glacier takes about a dozen seconds to return a sound after it lands. Images of evil spirits begin to torment him. High above the col, grotesque faces suddenly appear in the clouds, grimacing. Whymper trembles and briefly feels as if he is falling. He is ashamed of his fears. Is he really safe here on the saddle? Is danger not all around him? Rocks falling out of the fog, from the Tête du Lion, from the Matterhorn? Where are those overhanging rocks that could protect his bivouac?

Whymper basks in the sun briefly, which shines through a break in the clouds, and hears the Carrels somewhere above. He cannot see them. Are they somewhere on the ridge, or are they already on their way to the summit?

At noon, Whymper and his guide descend back to the cow shed, pack up their tent and other gear, and laboriously clamber back up to the col. Although heavily laden, they reach their bivouac before six o'clock in the evening.

Whymper's tent is made of light canvas and opens like a book. One end is closed permanently and the other end has flaps. It is supported by four alpenstocks, has canvas sides that turn in underneath, and is anchored by stones. Numerous cords are attached to the stones, and these and a rope that passes underneath the ridge and through iron rings screwed into the tops of the alpenstocks will allow the tent to withstand even strong winds.

So Whymper thinks. The tent collapses with the first gust of wind. It is obviously not made for such harsh conditions. Once the alpenstocks give in, the tarpaulin collapses. But Whymper does not give up. They will just have to make do without a tent. They sit on top of their equipment—nothing must blow away—and they wait. When night falls, they wrap themselves up in the canvas and make themselves as comfortable as the circumstances allow. When the wind drops, a majestic silence settles around them, and not a sound can be heard from the Carrels. Have they turned back? Or are they out of earshot?

All other creatures seem to have disappeared too. No falling rocks, not a breath of wind now, and it is bitterly cold. Their water bottles have turned into ice. Sleep is unthinkable, and so they wait. The thirst is nearly unbearable. At about midnight, they hear a tremendous explosion from high above. "Falling rocks!" one shouts. A great mass of rock is crashing toward them like artillery fire. They can hear it getting closer, and it feels like the end of the world, but then all goes silent again. The air is heavy with sulfur, and Whymper's heart races. At nature's mercy in situations such as this, fear is inevitable.

Finally, a clear day is dawning—the air flickers toward the south. Climbing in the shade, Whymper and his guide commence their ascent of the southwest ridge. Each handhold has to be firm, and each step has to be earned. This is genuine climbing. With every foot they gain in height, the abyss below them seems bigger. They are surrounded by mountains ruled by the three big peaks: Grivola, Gran Paradis, and Dent d'Hérens. All three can be seen at one glance. Even the pointed Monviso, nearly 100 miles (150 kilometers) away, is perfectly defined. With the ever-changing and steepening angle of the sun's rays, the shapes of the mountains alter. Soft lines suggesting a hidden crack suddenly disappear. Waves of drifted snow on a glacier sparkle briefly. Dark rock bands suddenly appear. And above it all, the vast expanse of the clear sky.

After about an hour, they arrive at the Chimney (Cheminée), the first difficult section above them. First they clamber over gravel, then zigzag up a lightly colored rock band and a slab of rock before they reach its first vertical step, a smooth intersection of two rocky gorges that are positioned at a considerable angle to one another. The guide examines the possibility of continuing. With his legs straddling rock, his fingers awkwardly jammed in cracks, advancing seems possible, but the guide is too tall to proceed here.

Whymper dares an attempt, however, and he succeeds. Now he stands on a platform looking up at the gray rock interspersed with brown stripes. He has come this far but now cannot pull up his companion, who is clumsy and too heavy. To Whymper's right, the rock steps seem climbable, the route manageable. If only his guide would follow!

"Come up!" he shouts, but he thinks, "What a coward!"

"I'd rather not!"

"Come up! I'll give you a tight rope!" Whymper tries to convince him.

"What for?"

"Because I want to go higher!"

"I don't! This is pointless!"

"Coward!" the Englishman calls out.

"Aren't you frightened?"

"No!"

"Big mouth!" the guide replies.

"Coward!" Whymper repeats.

"Carry on alone, then!"

"I'll do that! You go! Bugger off!"

"Fine! I'll descend by myself!"

"Yes, go back to Breuil!" Whymper shouts. "Tell them you have left your *monsieur* alone on the mountain."

"So what?"

"They won't understand!"

Whymper knows that a sense of honor requires guides to assist clients—if necessary, until the bitter end.

But when the guide starts his descent, Whymper loses his bravado. He begs his companion to come back and wait for him. Whymper does not want to advance much higher on his own, but the day has just begun, and there is no wind. There is no insuperable obstacle in sight. The gate to the summit seems wide open.

But what can he do alone on the Matterhorn? After all, he is not Jean-Antoine Carrel. Whymper gives in, loops the rope through an iron hook, which he attaches to the rock, and lowers himself down to his companion. With the assistance of his guide he descends to the col and returns with him to Breuil, where they arrive at about midday.

There is no sign of the Carrels, no news, not even rumors. Nobody in the valley knows where they are or where they have been. Have they advanced higher than before? How close did they come to the summit this time? Whymper later hears that one of them is said to have taken off his boots and tied them around his waist. Is it easier to climb difficult rocky passages barefoot? Apparently the one who climbed barefoot had lost one of his boots and had then descended to the Couloir du Lion with a length of cord wrapped around his foot. From here the two are said to have boldly glissaded all the way down to the valley. There is no news about a new record on La Gran Becca. No altitude readings, nothing—only the rumor about barefoot climbing. Whymper yearns for more information, anything that can help him in his next attempt.

The Matterhorn has risen in Whymper's estimation after this first attempt. The young Englishman leaves Breuil in 1861, convinced that Jean-Antoine Carrel was right to insist on a second guide. Alone with only one guide, single climbers do not get very far on the Matterhorn without risking their lives. For his next attempt, Whymper plans to take at least two guides—to back each other, if required. He suspects that a successful ascent will only be possible with Carrel. Whymper knows that Carrel is not only proud, he is also a strategist, and capable of anything. In any case, Carrel would be of good use to him.

He has to either win him over as his partner or else fear him as a rival. One or the other. In Whymper's eyes, Carrel is a perfect savage but does not think like a local mountain man. A hunter but one who acts like a city dweller.

When Whymper crosses the Col de Saint-Théodule to Zermatt on his way home, he decides he will continue his attempts on the Matterhorn until it is conquered. "It's either the mountain or me!" In this state of determination, more convinced of the scalability of the Matterhorn than ever before, he returns to London.

Carrel admires Whymper's toughness and climbing skills. He has observed him secretly and watched him climb. He also knows that Whymper's ambition is based largely on self-esteem for he hardly knows the mountain. Carrel, on the other hand, is more familiar with it than anyone. That is the source of his pride.

"Maybe I would have a chance if I teamed up with the Englishman," he reveals to his friends. "I want the ascent but not under his conditions."

Surely Whymper's stamina is admirable, but he lacks a clear overview as well as humility. He is naive and arrogant, a typical dandy. He has already written the story of his successful climb. It has all been predetermined. This makes him different from the locals.

"He talks too much," says Jean-Jacques Carrel back in the valley in autumn.

"Yes, he is a big mouth," Jean-Antoine replies.

"He lacks respect for the mountain."

"And experience."

"He just has a big mouth."

"Doesn't he just look like the Matterhorn? Cheeky, arrogant, and looking down from high above."

"Wearing his white pants and tiny hat, with the tent he carries around everywhere."

"La Gran Becca is an appropriate name for the mountain and for him."

Both break out laughing. In future, they will call him the Big Beak—but only if they are alone together.

CHAPTER 9

IN JANUARY 1862, THE FEARLESS mountaineer Thomas Stuart Kennedy from Leeds, England, launches an attempt on the Matterhorn from Zermatt, and he does so in the midst of winter. An unusual plan and an outlandish idea! Could the peak be climbed more easily in January than in July? Kennedy puts it to the test. Together with the guides Peter Perren and Peter Taugwalder he sets off from the valley despite large amounts of snow. They pass the night in the little chapel at the Schwarzsee and the next morning follow the route of the Parker brothers, accessing the mountain via the ridge between the north and east faces. Strong winds and frost soon force them to retreat. Silently they build a cairn of about six feet (1.8 meters) and place inside it a bottle containing a note bearing their names and the date. Then they descend to Zermatt as rapidly as possible and return to their lives. Kennedy later tells the locals of Zermatt, "The wind whirled up snow and hurled spicules of ice into our faces like needles. Flat pieces of ice a foot in diameter, carried up from the glacier below, went flying past. Still no one seemed to want to be the first to give in—until a gust even fiercer than usual forced us to shelter for a time behind a rock. Immediately it was tacitly understood that our expedition had ended."

In the summer of 1862, John Tyndall arrives for his second attempt to climb the Matterhorn. Born and raised in the Irish county of Carlow, Tyndall is twenty years Whymper's senior and an extraordinary scientist. It is his curiosity that drives him to the Alps year after year. He has worked with Michael Faraday, written sixteen books, and given countless lectures. And just as the famous researcher Tyndall is able to explain why the sky is blue, the recognized mountain pioneer Tyndall is keen to prove that there is a way to the summit of the Matterhorn. He left Breuil in August 1861, unable to make a second attempt, but this time he has come intent on completing his unfinished business with the mountain.

But Johann Bennen, who has studied the mountain from all sides on Tyndall's behalf, is skeptical.

"Impossible!" he says, expressing his honest opinion.

"And why exactly?" his brother Joseph wants to know.

"It's much more difficult and dangerous than expected."

"And if we fix the ascent route?"

"There are vertical passages, and there is no place upon it where we could pass the night."

"Not even on the Col du Lion?"

"We might do so, but there we should be almost frozen to death and totally unfit for the work of the next day."

"Not even higher up?"

"There are no ledges or crannies that could give us proper shelter on the Lion Ridge."

"And if we forego a bivouac?"

"Starting from Breuil it is certainly impossible to reach the summit in a single day."

Bennen is evidently against any attempt upon the mountain, and Tyndall is entirely taken aback by his report. There is also the rivalry between the guides from Zermatt and the ones from Valtournenche that makes Tyndall feel uncomfortable. He writes: "The Swiss are better at handling us noble gentlemen from England than the crude guides from the valley on the other side of the Matterhorn."

Tyndall remembers clearly how, during his attempt of 1860, his guide Bennen would constantly insult Jean-Jacques Carrel, the porter they engaged in Breuil: "I am the only one leading!" or "Be quiet!" The mood had hit rock-bottom. "He doesn't know a thing!" Bennen had barked. The men from the one side of the mountain cannot abide those from the other side having success in mountaineering or earning a guide's fee, Tyndall recalls. He is still appalled, even disgusted, at this.

Early in July 1862, Edward Whymper and Reginald Macdonald from England employ two local Zermatt guides, Johann zum Taugwald and Johann Kronig. Their intention to cross over to Breuil is thwarted by stormy weather, however. There is rain in the valleys, snow on the mountain.

Finally, on July 5, the party is able to cross the Col de Saint-Théodule. Just below the highest point, the air starts to crackle. Dense, black rain clouds race across the sky, but otherwise everything is still. An uncomfortable tension makes their hair stand on end and tugs at their bodies. Fearing that they might be struck by lightning, they rush across the pass and are happy to reach safety on the Italian side. When they find shelter in the inn at Breuil, away from the rain now roaring down, they can still feel the sensation of electric tension on their skin.

Whymper looks for a porter and on the advice of his landlord descends to the chalets of Breuil in search of a certain Luc Meynet. He finds a mean abode cluttered with cheese-making apparatus and some bright-eyed children who say that their uncle Luc will soon be home. A little later when a dark speck appears near an inconspicuous pine tree below the village, the children clap their hands and run eagerly down to greet their uncle and his mule. The ungainly, wobbly figure stoops down, picks up the little ones, and puts them into the empty panniers on each side of the mule. Luc Meynet, "the hunchback of Breuil," as he is called in the valley, approaches the noble Mr. Whymper, singing as he makes his way. He seems so at ease that it is as if he were not disabled—or at least that it did not affect his life.

"How may I help you, sir?" he asks.

"I would like to engage you as a porter."

"Where are you going?"

"Matterhorn."

"I have to look after my brother's children," Luc responds. His voice sounds hoarse.

"I understand."

"And I have to look after the cheese."

Eventually, Luc agrees to carry Whymper's tent up the mountain for a while. Whymper's new tent, rolled up, resembles a log, six feet long, weighing about twenty-two pounds. The tent can accommodate four people and has a base just under six feet square with equilateral triangles at both ends. It is supported by four ash-wood poles, each six-and-a-half-feet long and three inches in diameter at the base, tapering at the top to an inch and an eighth. The rope used for climbing also serves for the tent. It is passed over the crossed poles and underneath the ridge of the roof, and the two ends are secured to rock. It can be unrolled and set up by two people in three minutes, even in adverse weather.

Whymper is proud of his tent as it is custom-made and is the result of all his experience. Even though it is not completely waterproof, it offers adequate protection against wind, hail, and snow. Sir Leopold McClintock is said to have used a similar tent in the Arctic. It withstood the worst storms.

On July 7, a cloudless Monday, Whymper starts out with his party, and they pursue his route of the previous year. As none of his companions has been on the Matterhorn before, Whymper takes the lead. The party only becomes rebellious when he loses the way. While descending to get back on the right track, Kronig slips, screams, and slides past the others into the abyss.

The day seems lost, but before very long Kronig reappears, hunched and pale, aching all over, and the team continues the climb. Kronig remains speechless for one hour as Whymper continues to lead. The rocks towering above the Col du Lion are steep and snow-covered or varnished with ice. For this reason, Whymper sets up camp on the col. This time they do not pitch the tent directly on the snow but first collect a quantity of debris from the neighboring ledges. Flat rocks, earth, and mud form an insulating layer between the ice and the tent.

Luc Meynet turns out to be a pleasant fellow. He drinks the tail end of the coffee—the part with grounds in it—and takes the worst place, at the door of the tent. He has a sense of humor, does any kind of work, and even cleans up the camps without complaint. Like no other porter, he meets Whymper's expectations. Whymper detects a good climber too in this unusual man, making him a perfect companion.

A strong wind springs up from the east during the night and by morning it is almost a hurricane. The men inside the tent position themselves to hold it down, and this time the tent withstands the gales. After sunrise, a lull tempts them to head out, but they have hardly ascended a hundred feet before the storm bursts upon them with increased fury. Fist-sized rocks are flying and pieces of ice are being thrown into the air. It is intensely cold, the gales so strong that standing upright becomes impossible. Crouched behind a rocky outcrop, they wait for the storm to abate and then quickly retreat to their tent. Whymper's courage is shattered, the guides Taugwald and Kronig declare they have had enough of the Matterhorn, and Meynet also wants to retreat. He has some cheese-making commitments back home.

At the inn at Breuil, Whymper stumbles across Jean-Antoine Carrel, who has heard about the latest attempt and is curious how high the Englishmen was able to advance. Whymper, however, does not respond. He goes to his room leaving his ashamed guides and Meynet behind in the restaurant.

"How high?" Carrel asks the hunchback.

"Not far," Meynet replies.

"Because of the storm?"

"Yes, the wind."

"And the tent. Did it withstand the storm?"

"Yes. He left it on the col."

"And Whymper?"

"No problem."

When Whymper comes back to the restaurant, he looks Carrel directly in the eye.

"Do you want to come with me?"

"Is this an order?" Carrel smirks.

"No, a request."

"Right now?" Carrel wonders.

"Maybe tomorrow."

Carrel wants to take a second guide and a porter named Pession.

"On the first fine day, Macdonald and I want to leave, five of us with provisions for three days," Whymper says in a decisive tone.

Carrel does not say a word but knows exactly what he wants. He will make the decisions on the mountain. The English may be strong on foot, but they do not know the temperament of this mountain. In his view, the English are cowboys when it comes to climbing.

On July 9, at the crack of dawn, the party sets out in perfect weather, not a breath of wind, guides and porters leading the way. Carrel wants to pass the night as high up on the mountain as possible. He never walks too quickly, but his stride is steady and he advises the party not to take breaks. He is incredibly skilled, and his guiding is superior. Whymper trusts him completely. Without resting at the col, the party continues until they reach the top of the Tête du Lion. Near the foot of the Chimney, a little below the crest of the ridge on its eastern side, Carrel finds a protected place. By building up from ledge to ledge and connecting two rock steps with a dry wall, the guides construct a solid platform under Carrel's direction, as if he were a mason by profession.

"Other guides couldn't do that," Whymper praises him. Carrel does not say a word. He does not even talk to the other two guides, both from Switzerland, even though he knows that he is learning from them too.

The following day, Carrel leads the party higher up. After only an hour and a half of scrambling, they reach the ridge at the base of the Great Tower. Directly above them is only vertical rock. Can they dodge this bulwark to the right?

"What now?" Whymper asks.

"Tomorrow," Carrel simply says, and they return to their bivouac.

In perfect weather, with relatively high temperatures, Carrel scrambles up the Chimney the following day. Whymper and Macdonald follow without difficulty, but the porter Pession is unable to keep up. He is too tired and too weak. Carrel had an inkling about this and now sees the problem from high above. The man looks pale. Indeed, he looks very ill.

"I must go back!" Pession calls out hoarsely.

"Not on your own."

Carrel refuses to let the porter descend on his own. He feels responsible for everyone, including guides and porters. There is no way he would go on with the Englishmen alone.

"Pession is helpless and needs me," he tells Whymper.

"Whymper and I could try to get higher without a guide," Macdonald says.

"This is out of the question," says Carrel.

He knows that without him they would be lost higher up and orders them to retreat. It is either everyone up or everyone down.

"Can we not just look around the next corner?" Whymper begs. "Why not?"

"Not under my leadership. This is irresponsible."

And so the party returns to Breuil, and the following day Macdonald leaves. He has to go back to London.

For the third time, Whymper has failed on the Matterhorn. He did not even get one step higher than the highest point reached by his guide. However, nobody really knows how high Carrel has actually been on the mountain. It remains a mystery. Whymper is now convinced that up to the altitude of nearly 13,000 feet (4,000 meters) there are no extraordinary difficulties on the Matterhorn. The sheer walls above the last 1,800 feet (500 meters) look absolutely terrifying, however. Here a modest rock seven feet tall might defeat the best climbing party, if it were perpendicular. If need be, two people can secure each other on such sections. Three people can even use short wooden ladders or poles. But getting a sick or injured person down that mountain seems unthinkable. This is why Carrel refuses to go unless the party consists of at least four people. Absolutely! The higher up, the more dangerous the climbing, simply because rescues are increasingly difficult at high altitude.

Jean-Antoine Carrel is not the only guide who thinks like that. Many Swiss guides refuse to work on the Horu (the Swiss guides' name for the Matterhorn) not only because they do not believe that it is scalable; they simply do not want to die there. There is certainly a lack of people like Carrel, who are prepared to take the risk as well as the full responsibility. Whymper, feeling left in the lurch by Carrel, now goes to Zermatt to find a willing guide there. Yet again! And during a stormy week, he climbs Monte Rosa.

Chapter 10

On July 17, Whymper is back in Breuil, this time without a guide. The Hörnli Ridge, which he looked at when he came across from Switzerland, seems unclimbable to him. So once again he wants to launch an attempt from the Italian side, working with local guides. He now knows the ascent route like the back of his hand. Jean-Antoine Carrel and Luc Meynet, neither of whom are full-time guides, are inclined to go, but their occupations prevent them from starting at once. Or so they say. Whymper thinks he will be all right on his own, with his tent still rolled up and left behind at the second platform, but he wonders whether it blew away during recent stormy weather.

On July 18, he heads out on his own and, to the astonishment of herdsmen watching, makes very quick progress.

The real climbing begins high above the pastures, though. Here the lone mountaineer slows down and tries to memorize every landmark. He may need these to find his way down again, in case of fog. Climbing alone, Whymper finds his skills put to the test and experiences strange fears, and all of a sudden he becomes his own observer, just as

Carrel would watch him climb. He can now sense Carrel's worries and the dual responsibility he has for his client and himself. If you have to rely entirely on your own legs and make your own decisions, you have to pay attention to every small detail in order to minimize risk. High up on the mountain, every move can be a matter of life and death.

Whymper first gauges his altitude according to the snowline and later by the surrounding peaks. He notices landmarks he has never paid any attention to before. He recognizes his limits and at the same time realizes that he might better his past achievements. He alternates between utter concentration on his handholds and footholds, which he needs when climbing some of the passages, and amazement at the vegetation he sees, the incredible variety of grasses, flowers, and moss, which must have been living here for thousands of years: various kinds of saxifrages, gentians, *Linaria alpina*, *Thlaspi rotundifolium*. The plants also try to climb higher and higher, even though most of their attempts fail.

Whymper finds his tent without difficulty, although it is snow-covered. For the lone climber, the view is magical up here. The sky is completely clear, and the Breithorn, Lyskamm, Monte Rosa, and summits of the Graian Alps and the Pennine chain appear as if the setting of a divine global stage. In the far distance he sees the pyramid of Monte Viso. Right in front of him stands the Dent d'Hérens, its north face shaded and interspersed with enormous hanging glaciers that sometimes break away in immense slices and thunder down on the Tiefenmatten Glacier. Farther right soars the Dent Blanche, which from his perspective is the most beautiful of all mountains. The Matterhorn, on the other hand, has been reduced to an indistinguishable wall of rock from where he is standing.

Blinded by the setting sun, Whymper sets up his tent. As he has brought provisions for several days and the temperature is favorable, he has decided to stay overnight on the mountain. Nobody will worry about him in Breuil. From his tent door, triangular like the silhouette of the Matterhorn, he watches the twilight change to darkness. The view seems like an ever-changing painting, and the spectacle is almost divine. Is he the only person with the privilege of having experienced this? He watches and waits until the moon rises, when he can begin to make out the silhouettes of the mountains, and slowly the surfaces gain depth and structure. The world around him seems more powerful than during the day—and so vast, with a silence that permeates everything. Whymper is neither atheistic nor religious, but he is affected by this beauty. Under moonlight, the mountains sparkle like giant crystals in space.

In the morning he makes coffee, enjoys the comfort of his tent for a while, and sets out at sunrise when he starts to get cold. Tempted by the brilliant weather, he proceeds yet higher in search of another place for a platform.

But his solitary scrambling up this giant vertical space frightens him and makes him hesitate, and the ascent becomes harder with every step. The technical difficulties present one challenge, but even greater is the feeling of being alone. Finding the way is also becoming more difficult. Is it true that he does not have Jean-Antoine Carrel's instinct for the terrain? Whymper stays aware of the dangers and tries to convince himself of the sufficiency of his technical equipment: the tent, his ice axe, and a claw—a kind of grapnel—to which he can fix the rope with which to lower himself if necessary. Wherever the holds are too small or nonexistent, he attaches the claw to a ledge, examines its grip properly, threads the rope through the ring at its end, and lowers himself carefully, keeping the rope taut to prevent the claw from slipping off the rock.

Despite his feelings of insecurity, Whymper climbs higher. He sometimes follows the southern (Breuil) side of the ridge, and sometimes he turns over to the northern (Zermatt) side. The rock consists of sloping steps, each as much as a few hundred feet high. Finally, Whymper reaches the foot of the Great Tower, the highest point attained by Hawkins and Tyndall two years ago, a possible place to camp.

Beyond the Great Tower, which protrudes from the ridge like the turret of a gigantic castle, he glimpses rocky pinnacles that stand out significantly against the blue sky. "How difficult will it be to get there?" Whymper wonders. The perfect weather and his curiosity spur him on. He advances higher on the right of the Great Tower, ascending cliffs, locates a suitable place to pitch his tent, and then, enticed by the daylight that is left, goes on to see what the vertical world behind the tower looks like. Always keeping to the right, he crosses ramps and reaches a gap between two rocky spurs. From here he cannot see the summit pyramid.

Whymper takes a deep breath. He gazes down into the void to his left and right, and the small ridge above him seems to sway. He looks away from the abyss and scrambles up steep walls to advance higher. Once, he must jump to find a handhold. Then his feet dangle in the air, and by sheer strength he hauls himself up over the sharp rocks.

The distance down to the Tiefenmatten Glacier seems monstrous, and the route leading right around a second tower looks terrifying. Several times Whymper finds himself in a position where handholds are so tenuous that his fingers threaten to slip off. Climbing is barely possible. Would it not be better to turn back? Routefinding takes time, his hands are now bloody, and his knees are shaking. On ledges that taper off, he now clambers up a steep gully to the right of a jagged ridge and sometimes finds himself with arms and legs spread, as if crucified. His body pressed against the rock, he feels each rise and fall of his chest as he breathes. Now he looks around for a hold but cannot see any. Farther to his left he sees a rocky pinnacle as high as a church tower, which looks ready to drop into the void. The view paralyzes him, and he turns from it to concentrate on his handholds and footholds. Part gymnast and part aerialist, he is now driven by exhilaration and fear that have merged into one. Is he still in control of his climbing, or has he crossed the line separating the possible from the impossible?

Whymper knows that he must not go beyond his abilities. That would be irresponsible—and perhaps fatal. But his desire to be better than his peers overrides any perceived limitation of his own abilities. Has he already gone higher than his rivals? He needs to come down the way he came up—either by climbing or lowering himself.

Still climbing upward, the route becomes easier for a time, leading him across some solid rocky slabs and decayed ruins, but everywhere scree is ready to fall. The rock, a talcose gneiss, is cleft, the mountain hacked by rough weather. Whymper stands on a ridge, in the notch between two tottering pillars, with only the abyss to his left and right. Above him: more strange and rugged rock formations, gnomes with monstrous grins, rocky debris, isolated towers that seem ready to fall.

Whymper is aware of the destructive effect of frost, and he accepts that continuing to climb on this loose rock would be too dangerous, even impossible for him. He has climbed pretty high, though! Whymper looks across the central Pennine Alps all the way to the Grand Combin, with the Mont Blanc massif behind. The Dent d'Hérens, the Matterhorn's immediate neighbor, still rises above him but not by much.

It is here that Whymper decides to climb down. He lowers himself in places, leaves his tent and ice axe behind, and hurries back toward Breuil in twilight. At the Col du Lion—only about fifty more steps till reaching the Great Staircase, which he wants to descend before darkness—he hesitates. At the edge of the cliffs leading toward the Tête du Lion, the steps he cut during his ascent have disappeared. The warmth of the day has turned the snowfield into a sheet of ice, and his tracks have gone. The rocks beyond the snowfield seem climbable, but he will have to cut steps to get there. The snow is very hard, topped with glittering ice. Holding onto rock with his right hand, Whymper uses the point of his alpenstock to cut steps.

Everything seems to go well, but when he turns around he slips and falls, and suddenly he is sliding down the steep snowfield in a gully that leads from the Glacier du Lion between two rock buttresses. Helpless, he still is clear-minded and aware that he could easily tumble another three hundred meters. Picking up speed where the gully gets narrower, Whymper approaches a small gap between two rock walls. Below this he can see only a void and the glacier farther down. Unable to break his fall, Whymper is whirling now across ice and rocks. His alpenstock is dashed from his hand, and plummeting headfirst, he strikes his head on rocks as he is catapulted from one edge of the gully to the other. Finally, the left side of his body collides with rocks that bring him to a halt.

Whymper, now teetering on the edge of a precipice, raises his head and watches as his alpenstock and hat skim past him and disappear. He must have fallen around two hundred feet (sixty meters). A few more and he would have been dead. He is not upset with himself, but for a moment he thinks about Jean-Antoine Carrel. What would the guide say about such foolhardiness?

It is a miracle that Whymper is still alive. He is badly injured, though: his head, his hands, his whole body. He tries to stop the most serious bleeding with handfuls of snow. With each heartbeat, blood gushes out of his head wounds. In shock, the injured climber scrambles back to the safety of the ridge, and there he faints.

The sun has already set when Whymper comes to. Nevertheless, he descends the 4,800 feet (1,500 meters) down to Breuil without falling or getting lost, proceeding as if in a trance.

"I was perfectly conscious of what was happening," Whymper will write later in *Scrambles Amongst the Alps,*

> and felt each blow; but, like a patient under chloroform, experienced
> no pain. Each blow was, naturally, more severe than that which
> preceded it, and I distinctly remember thinking "Well, if the next is
> harder still, that will be the end!" Like persons who have been rescued
> from drowning, I remember that the recollection of a multitude of
> things rushed through my head, many of them trivialities or absurdi-
> ties, which had been forgotten long before; and, more remarkable, this
> bounding through space did not feel disagreeable. But I think that in
> no very great distance more, consciousness as well as sensation would
> have been lost, and upon that I base my belief, improbable as it seems,
> that death by a fall from a great height is as painless an end as can be
> experienced.

"Maybe for the dead person," Jean-Antoine Carrel muses when he hears the story. "But what about the people left behind?"

CHAPTER 11

IN BREUIL, JEAN-ANTOINE CARREL LEARNS more details about Whymper's accident. He is surprised by Whymper's fall, perhaps, but not by Whymper's cool-headed take on his experience or by the altitude he reached.

While Whymper is hiding out for a few days, recovering from his injuries and thinking about the vanity of his desires, details about his fall on the Matterhorn spread like wildfire. From house to house, from person to person.

"The only serious effect has been the reduction of a naturally retentive memory to a very commonplace one," Whymper will later write, "and although my recollections of more distant occurrences remain unshaken, the events of that particular day would be clean gone but for the few notes which were written down before the accident."

Whymper does not want to lose time. On July 23, four days after his near-death experience descending solo, he is already en route on another attempt, this time with two guides as well as Luc Meynet. Carrel's decision to join the Englishman is based solely on the desire to verify how high Whymper actually advanced on July 19. He wants to keep control over all attempts on his mountain! This time they climb the Great Tower in brilliant sunshine, without meeting with any difficulty, when suddenly mist forms out of nowhere. After a few minutes, it starts to snow and sleet. They stay put for several hours, hoping and shivering. Finally, when the storm is over, they descend to the base of the Great Tower, make a platform, and set up camp for the night. They take refuge in the tent while it starts to snow again.

"The weather won't improve," Carrel remarks.

"Are you sure?" Whymper asks.

Carrel is worried: "I am sure that the mountain will be glazed with ice in the morning."

"Any further attempts would be in vain?"

"Completely!"

"It happens quite frequently that there are brief thunderstorms up here while the sun is shining down in the valley," Whymper points out.

"High up on the mountain, you need good visibility and fine weather."

Whymper puts his hand on the ground. "The rock is warm; it won't ice up soon." He wants to wait and see.

Carrel insists on going down; he does not tolerate resistance. "Up here I make the decisions, and your safety is more important to me than the summit."

They head back and below the col they step out of the thick fog and gaze down into a sun-flooded valley. Only the Matterhorn is covered in cloud, with brilliant blue sky and sunshine all around it. Whymper does not say a word, but thinks to himself: "Carrel is certainly not an easy man to manage."

Carrel's decision to descend is not only based on his ambition to be the first man to conquer the Matterhorn and to do it his own way. It's also based on his feeling that Whymper is too young for such an undertaking.

Carrel plays his own game and does not conceal it from Whymper. He does not need the Englishman, and money means less to him than the mountain. It does not matter whether Whymper simply wants him to come along or pays him for it. He only wants to acquire a monopoly on the Matterhorn. Whymper, on the other hand, sees in Carrel his only chance to reach the summit. He cannot quite comprehend his behavior, but he knows that Carrel's unpredictability is not based on cowardice. After all, nobody can blame a mountain guide for feeling too responsible, no matter how stubborn he is. Carrel's reason for turning back has never been that the route was too difficult, and his desire to reach the summit is obvious. When it comes to his role as a guide, Carrel takes Whymper's climbing abilities as a measure for what the pair can actually achieve on the mountain. The Englishman, however, is too arrogant to notice that his skills are the limiting factor. Carrel's people, on the contrary, who grew up at the base of the mountain, know instinctively how far they can go. They certainly have more potential to climb the Matterhorn than the city dweller, who has only been coming to the Alps sporadically for three years. However, the two men would still make the perfect team on the mountain. Whymper bears the cost and Carrel, the responsibility. This happens quite naturally, without either of them having to think or talk about it. Carrel has always been more interested in his clients' abilities than his own fee. He never demands too much and always commits to one tour at a time along with pay.

Back in the valley, Whymper is vexed at having lost time. But Carrel promises they will set out again the following day.

"We will climb to the foot of the tower and fix some rope in the most difficult places beyond it," he suggests.

Whymper is enthusiastic: "And then attack the summit from high camp?"

But the following morning only Meynet, the hunchback, waits for the Englishman.

"The two Carrels have gone off to catch marmots," the porter says, making excuses for them.

"To hell with those creatures."

"The weather is favorable for hunting."

"These men clearly cannot be relied upon," Whymper rages. He proposes that the hunchback accompany him anyway, just one more time before Whymper's holidays come to an end.

"I want to try to reach the summit," Whymper says.

"Not a chance."

"Why so negative?"

"Reaching the summit without Jean-Antoine is impossible."

After only a few hours the pair stands upon the Col du Lion.

Meynet falls to his knees, claps his hands a few times, and exclaims with tears in his eyes: "Oh, beautiful mountains!" Silent and humble, he remains in this position like a praying monk. They advance to the southwest ridge, pass the night in the tent at the old campsite below the Great Tower, and set out very early the following day. They quickly pass the place where they had turned back previously and reach an almost vertical wall. On sloping hand-holds they climb up a cliff to a notch from which any progress is impossible. There is no way forward and no way back. Beyond the notch in the ridge, the sky opens, and an abyss looms below. They are stuck! Like two eagles with drooping wings they remain at the same spot on the rock for a while.

"What to do?" Meynet is at a loss.

"Go back!" Whymper's realization comes a little late. Too late?

He decides to return to Breuil to have a light wooden ladder made to assist them over some of the steepest parts on their next attempt.

"And who shall carry the ladder?" Meynet wonders.

"Carrel."

They lower themselves down the difficult sections. With his legs dangling in the air, Meynet does not take his eyes off Whymper and remains cheerful as he usually does on the most difficult parts of a climb. "We can only die once," he jokes. Back in the valley, he tells Carrel about an insurmountable vertical wall above the big snowfield.

CHAPTER 12

IN THE MEANTIME, PROFESSOR TYNDALL has arrived back in Breuil with three Valaisan guides in tow, Johann Bennen and Anton Walter among them. He does not mention his plans to Whymper. Carrel and his relative César also keep quiet, but the two men have not been idle. They have constructed a ladder, collected provisions, and joined Professor Tyndall's party to climb the mountain. Whymper is more than disappointed about Carrel's disloyalty, especially because of the ladder—after all, it was his idea. He feels betrayed, even tricked. Does he feel defeated too? Maybe, for he knows that without Carrel he does not stand a chance to compete against Tyndall.

Nevertheless, Whymper and the hunchback set out from Breuil for the Col du Lion at noon, following Tyndall's party. He wants to recover some of his equipment from his tent. Just below the col he overtakes the slow team of the professor. He certainly does not admire the professor's style, but he envies him for Carrel. At the Col du Lion, Whymper and Meynet hear a singing noise coming from above. When they look up, they see a rock the size of a head flying toward them. Quickly they dive under a large outcrop just in time to avoid the whooshing missile. A loud roar follows, and more rocks—indeed, rock avalanches—tumble down, leaving a trail of dust and sulfur behind.

At the camp, Whymper waits for the professor, briefly salutes him, and then goes back down to Breuil. When Whymper is packing the next morning to return to England, some of the villagers come running and pointing to the Matterhorn.

"They're on the top!"

"Where?"

"Where the flag flies."

Whymper looks through his binoculars and then breathes a sigh of relief. The party stands atop the shoulder and not on the summit of his mountain. Tyndall may have gone beyond the point where he and Meynet had been forced to turn back, but he has not reached the goal. It is still a long and difficult way from the shoulder to the real summit, with the last cliff somewhat overhanging.

As he wants to weigh his prospects, Whymper waits for his rivals to return before he departs. He drinks a parting glass of wine with Favre and promises him to return.

When the six climbers amble down across the pastures, there is no spring in their steps. They too have been defeated. Carrel's head is bowed, and the others complain that the mountain is horrible, impossible, and so forth. Even Professor Tyndall, who says they were within a stone's throw of the summit, is now convinced: the Matterhorn is unscalable. He will not dare another attempt. Whymper, on the contrary, has left his rope and tent in the hands of the innkeeper. He'll come back and use them again next year.

With his announced conviction that the Matterhorn is unscalable, Tyndall, who has made mountaineering accessible to a broader public, has further fueled Whymper's burning desire. He not only wants to bolster his own image but also the image of the English Crown. The wish to cement the impression of England as a country of conquering heroes drives him as much as the Matterhorn does. Inspired by the adventures of English polar explorers Ross and Franklin, he wants to shine and become a national hero like each of them. The distinguished circle of the London-based Alpine Club, however, deems this kind of mountaineering—a sport without scientific elements—suspicious. They are especially irritated by Whymper's solo attempts. Tyndall can only shake his head in amazement. This is a young fellow who has just learned how to climb, who plunges unprepared into new adventures, dares to go higher and higher, and then wants to climb the Matterhorn solo.

Whymper is convinced that with Jean-Antoine Carrel he can definitely reach the summit. He could then earn his living with wood engravings—a craft his father taught him—and later publish his heroic tales along with his illustrations in a picture book. If Jean-Antoine would only be loyal to him!

Carrel made an impression on Whymper from the very beginning: his independence, his resolution, the provoking air around him—that is what he likes! Only Carrel's disloyalty offends him. Whymper has repeatedly proposed to him that they tackle the mountain together, just the two of them. The Swiss guides—to hell with their reputation—are just not interested in climbing the Matterhorn!

Carrel wants to be independent and in control. He watches every step of the intruder, Whymper, and acts like a hunter, not like a warrior. With Tyndall he reached a point higher than Whymper had climbed. Had Whymper continued his solo ascent earlier in the month, no doubt Carrel would have scrambled ahead of him and reached the top first. His ambivalent behavior toward Whymper, his apparent wavering between respect and dominance, is in his nature. His passion for climbing does not quite match Whymper's ambition to be the first to reach the summit, and they both want to lead, to make the decisions, but they belong together. They both want to conquer the Matterhorn.

"Tyndall climbed higher than I did," Whymper thinks. But it was only with the assistance of a ladder that they were able to surmount the most difficult section on the mountain, and this section is exactly where he had left rope during his descent—as a climbing aid for the next time. He intends to eventually use it.

The Matterhorn is to Whymper what Mont Blanc was to Jacques Balmat (the man who completed the first recorded ascent of Mont Blanc on August 8, 1786): the center of his life. He aspires to succeed at any cost, not just for himself but also for his countrymen. Step by step, enduring pain, he has reconnoitered an ascent route over two years. For a whole winter, Whymper thinks about Jean-Antoine Carrel and the Matterhorn. Could Carrel have actually taken Tyndall to the top? Maybe, but Whymper knows Carrel's character and is convinced that he would not have wanted to share the summit success with a Swiss guide. Even though Carrel respects Bennen, who for his part despises Italian guides, he would have never helped Bennen reach the top.

The Valtournenchians' aversion toward the inhabitants of the neighboring valley is deeply rooted. Carrel worries that one of them will snatch his summit away from him. The language barrier is an obstacle. Bennen only speaks German, and apart from his local dialect, Carrel only speaks French. In any case, Carrel is not given to following orders, whether from an English client or another guide. He wants to climb the Matterhorn, but he refuses to be subordinate to anyone. When Tyndall had asked him whether it was possible to proceed from the shoulder just below the summit, Carrel had replied: "Sir, please ask your guide. I am only your porter." In Whymper's view, this reflects Carrel's character. In Tyndall's attempt on the Matterhorn it was Bennen who failed as a guide, not Carrel who failed as a climber.

CHAPTER 13

WHEN THE ENGLISH ALPINE CLUB appeals to its members to persevere in attempts at the first ascent of the Matterhorn, a handful of Italian mountain enthusiasts gather in the San Valentino Castle in Piedmont to discuss the foundation of their own alpine club. It is July 1863. On this occasion they also set a secret goal: to climb the Matterhorn from the Italian side. The Club Alpino Italiano (CAI) intends to bring honor to the young kingdom of Italy, and its members know that English alpinists beat the Italians in becoming the first to scale Monviso in the Piedmont. The only peak in the Western Alps left for the Italians is the Matterhorn. For the first time, Alpinism has clearly become a matter of national pride, setting the tone for the next hundred years.

The members of the CAI include such highly motivated scientists and skilled and wealthy scholars as Quintino Sella, Bartolomeo Gastaldi, Felice Giordano, Benedetto Rignon, and Perrone di San Martino. They know about the various attempts of the Valtournenche guides, who have prepared the route for many years. But simply preparing a route is not enough. A successful undertaking requires money, a plan, logistics, and a coordinator, and Felice Giordano is asked to take on the responsibility. They are running out of time. The establishment of the Club Alpino is due to be made public on October 23, 1863, and it should coincide with an Italian victory on the Matterhorn.

In August 1863, Whymper is back in Breuil, like a migratory bird. His first move is to find Jean-Antoine Carrel.

"You don't want to give up, do you?" Carrel says.

"I can't."

"And why do you come to me?"

"With you, there is hope. Without you, there is none."

"Unfortunately, I can't come this time," Carrel responds.

Carrel knows that Whymper depends on him. He does not want to raise the Englishman's hopes, and he does have other commitments. There is friction between the two, but they agree on one thing: they do not climb primarily for a club or a nation. The Matterhorn is their own personal business.

Carrel agrees to a training excursion around the Matterhorn: from Valtournenche to Zermatt and the Valpelline and then back to Breuil. Whymper's stamina on this excursion so impresses Carrel that he agrees to attempt the Matterhorn with the Englishman again, but Carrel only has three days to spare. They agree to start from Giomein, above Breuil.

"We only go if the weather is favorable," Carrel says.

Whymper gives Carrel carte blanche in planning the route and choosing the guides. Jean-Antoine wrangles César Carrel, Luc Meynet, and two porters. On Sunday, August 9, the weather is clearing, the mist around the mountaintops disappearing, and the party starts just before dawn the following day, which begins cool and cloudless. Reaching the rock just a few hundred feet below the Col de Saint-Théodule, they find it both varnished with ice and covered with some loose snow. When Jean-Antoine examines the ground with his ice axe and begins to cut steps, the slope upon which he stands breaks, and masses of snow come toward him. Jean-Antoine jumps, turning in the air, and manages to land without falling, then secures himself.

"It's about time we roped up," he remarks.

Once they are tied on the rope, Jean-Antoine continues to lead.

Whymper does not say a word. They continue as if nothing happened.

The pace is slow but steady. Traversing to the Col du Lion, the climbers find it covered in ice and sharper than the ridge of a church roof. On this occasion, Whymper appreciates the climbing rope but only if it is kept tight between him and the guides. A slip on the ice won't be followed by a fall if both people in front and behind hold him. The meltwater from the previous day has covered the rocks with a film of paper-thin ice. With his experience, Jean-Antoine climbs carefully ahead and scrapes the ice off handholds and footholds. Whymper, who feels completely safe in Jean-Antoine's care, is nevertheless grateful for the safety rope.

At the base of the Great Tower, the climbers are hit by an icy wind. It is difficult to say where the gusts come from, and Jean-Antoine senses that this is not an ordinary wind. The air feels heavier than usual. At one moment it seems to descend from higher up, then it goes completely tranquil again, with not a speck of cloud in the sky. All of a sudden mists form around the south side of the mountain and elsewhere above and below them. A few snowflakes fall.

"A snowstorm is brewing," Jean-Antoine says.

"How long will it last?" asks Whymper.

"If it comes from the east, it will bring a lot of snow."

The ridge is covered in snow in no time.

"What to do?" asks Whymper.

"Monsieur," Jean-Antoine replies, "the weather changes quickly up here."

"So suddenly?"

"Sometimes it's a matter of minutes," César laughs.

"I didn't ask for your opinion," Whymper snaps.

"Why not?" Jean-Antoine says.

"When will it improve?"

"Who knows," Jean-Antoine says calmly. "This is a good place for our camp. Let's stop here."

"If we continue, we will freeze to death," says Meynet.

Nobody disagrees with him. The guides make a platform for the tent and pitch it. The clouds darken.

The five men sit inside the tent as the thunderstorm breaks upon them. Lightning shoots down at the rocks, and roaring thunder shakes the mountain. Whymper is afraid of getting scorched. Now the thunder is nearly simultaneous with the lightning, a flash and a crash together. The storm lasts for nearly two hours, the thunder and its echoes immediately followed by new thunderclaps. The wind blows from the east, a gale, and even though the tent is weighed down by their bodies and protected by rocks, Whymper fears they might get blown away. During a lull, the guides venture out to build a protective wall against the wind, which at some point changes to the northwest, forcing the clouds to move away. A little later they can see the sunset just behind the Mont Blanc range. What a splendid spectacle! And what a feeling: as if they were the only survivors of the apocalypse.

Tucked in their blankets inside the tent, they pass the night comfortably enough, but there is little chance of sleeping. It is not just the adrenaline of having survived a storm, but also the frequent crash of falling rocks. Whymper is certain that the most significant rockfalls usually occur just before daybreak, but the sound of falling rocks is most frightening in the darkness.

When early morning snow ceases, Jean-Antoine wants to continue up toward the shoulder. But being familiar with the terrain above the Great Tower, Whymper is concerned that an attempt would not be possible under these circumstances, with the heavy baggage—tent, blankets, provisions, ladder, and 450 feet (120 meters) of rope. They unanimously agree to turn back as they have not even reached the rope that Tyndall's party left attached to the vertical rock just below the shoulder. At one point, Jean-Antoine slowly lowers everyone individually.

The men get back to Breuil in the course of the afternoon—in the finest weather. People at the inn are astonished to learn that the party was exposed to a twenty-four-hour snowstorm.

"We didn't see a spot of rain," Favre says.

"The devil was raging up there. I thought we were sitting in hell," Whymper says.

"How is this possible?"

"The mountain is cursed."

Carrel smiles to himself and walks away. In his mind, wind, snow, and sudden drops in temperature are part of the mountain. Heaven only becomes hell when people have false expectations.

"Was there really no thunderstorm during our absence?" Whymper asks again after the guides have left.

"It has been fine all the time."

"Not a cloud in the sky?"

"There was a small cloud on the mountain and some clouds gathered on the south face, with wafts of fog creeping up the valley. But that was it."

This time Whymper feels tricked by the insidious clouds and not by Carrel for a change. Due to the natural occurrence of the Matterhorn warming up every day, because of its altitude and its location, clouds gather around it. This happens especially in good weather, on calm days when the temperature fluctuates. Humidity from rising air condenses more rapidly in some spots than others. When warm rising air meets cold air, fog gathers. Once it thickens, a thunderstorm breaks out between the two layers of air with different temperatures.

Whymper ruminates a lot about these natural phenomena—he is very inquisitive. But first and foremost he is a mountaineer. He has tried to reach the summit seven times now, always via the ridge leading up from Breuil. And each time the Matterhorn has rejected him. Once again he is bidding goodbye like a gambler who has lost everything.

Carrel is convinced that Whymper will be eager to have another go the next summer in the belief that he will finally win. Luck must be on his side for once, and in London he will have time to form a plan for that next summit attempt. Whymper has no inkling that Carrel will not be his man the next time.

Chapter 14

In 1865, there are ten qualified mountain guides in Zermatt. Their guests are from Switzerland, Germany, and France, but they are first and foremost from England. Guiding clients to the top of Monte Rosa has become routine, especially for Peter Taugwalder. At the age of forty-four, he has reached its summit ninety times. Forty-year-old Matthäus Zumtaugwald, who was on Ueli Lauener's team during the first ascent in 1855 and has stood atop Monte Rosa forty times, is second in the ranking. Also in the hall of fame are the well-travelled Peter Perren, the youngest guide; Franz Biner, also known as Weisshorn-Biner; Johann and Stephan Zumtaugwald, the two younger brothers of the famous Matthäus; and Mont Blanc expert Johann Kronig, who is said to communicate with English clergymen in Latin. These men do not work together in a guides' union; each one of them negotiates his fees with clients individually. They draw from years of experience to evaluate their clients' abilities and find the right excursions for them.

It is not the mountain guides who are struggling to gain power in Zermatt at this time but more the local pastor, Father Josef Ruden, as well as the hotel owner Alexander Seiler. Seiler comes from outside the valley, and the tourists believe everything he says. Meanwhile every word Ruden preaches in his sermons is sacred to the locals of Zermatt. Because the pastor speaks against an ascent of the Matterhorn, Taugwalder does not dare explore the Hörnli-Ridge, let alone scale the Horu. But deep down he believes that the mountain is scalable and is probably the only person in Zermatt to think so.

The Valais has become a mecca for serious alpinists. The first president of the Alpine Club, the famous botanist John Ball, sings the praises of Zermatt. He calls it the Eldorado for true mountaineers. Getting there is not that easy for travelers from afar. After a long coach ride through the Rhone Valley and a seven-hour hike through the Matter Valley, a mule track stretching over thirty miles (forty-five kilometers), the travelers finally reach their destination. For the common tourist this undertaking is usually too strenuous, which is why it deters typical hikers from Zermatt but attracts real alpinists.

On the other side of the mountain, the people of Valtournenche look at the arrival of tourism differently. It seems they are afraid of strangers. This outlook dates back to the days when the Valtournenchians and the Valaisans were rivals and a boundary wall on the Col Theodule separated the two communities. The locals of Valtournenche started to erect barricades to defend themselves against the continuous attacks by the people of the Valais. And with the rise of alpinism, this animosity seems to continue. The mountain guides of the Italian side of the Matterhorn consider their fellow guides from Zermatt intruders.

The people of Valtournenche think all foreigners are English, even if they are German or French. When Quintino Sella scales the Breithorn in 1854, his guide actually introduces him to locals as "The Englishman from Biella." These guides are truly peculiar fellows. With their local pride and farmers' dignity, they approach tourists with an arrogant subservience that must make a strange impression.

The Zermatt guides also started off as simple people. They were once naive peasants. Even though they were only engaged as porters, they led tourists across icy stretches and cut steps for them, for they were significantly stronger than their urban clients. Having earned some extra money as luggage carriers and pathfinders, they soon considered themselves guides, for they not only knew the way, they were also more skillful in the high mountains than those who hired them.

The Chamonix guides, who are very well known and feel superior to all their peers in the Alps, view the young men from Valtournenche as no better than porters. Especially when it comes to their pay. The famous guides from Chamonix—Michel Payot, Jean Tairraz, Michel Croz, Gédeon Balmat, and Jean-Pierre Cachat—are by no means more accomplished climbers than Carrel, but they are much more accomplished at dealing with the peculiarities of their clients. But soon the guides from Valtournenche also earn their respect, and it does not take long for some tourists to hire them, rather than guides from Zermatt. Among them are Joseph Bich, one of the oldest guides; Augustin Pelissier; Antoine Gorret (Amé Gorret's father); Pierre and Gabriel Maquignaz, and above all, Jean-Antoine Carrel, the passionate hunter and climber who accompanied Tyndall all the way to the shoulder of the Matterhorn in August 1862.

Jean-Antoine Carrel! He served in the 1849 Battle of Gran Novara in the First Italian War of Independence, fought Radetzky's army atop the hills of San Marino, and now, back at the foot of the Matterhorn, has become a sought-after mountain guide. Carrel acts of his own accord. Even though he knows that all high mountains bear great dangers, he is neither crazy nor motivated by money. His dream is to conquer the Matterhorn. He does not need an explanation for this desire. He simply wants to be the first person to reach the summit, and he aspires to achieve it with locals from his valley. Under his guidance he has formed a small group of local guides who trust each other and share their love for the mountains. They are herdsmen, hunters, and smugglers and keep up their professions even when they work as mountain guides. Being used to a simple lifestyle, seemingly uncouth to outsiders, the mountain dwellers likewise initially react suspiciously toward tourists coming to their valley from faraway places. The guides cannot gauge their wealth, but they can eventually judge their true characters, which appear with the first thunderstorm on the mountain or during difficult stretches of climbing. Toward the mountain the locals are humble and respectful, an attitude toward nature that has been nurtured since childhood. Their local pride has nothing to do with egotism or idealism, but everything to do with personal responsibility.

By now, two inns have opened on the Swiss side of the mountain in Zermatt: the Monte Rosa, managed by Alexander Seiler, and the Mont Cervin, owned by Josef Anton Clemenz. Their clientele are mainly young fellows from the English upper class who want to compete in mountaineering and who see scaling one of the highest summits in the Alps as a particularly noble kind of conquest.

CHAPTER 15

IN THE SUMMER OF 1864, things seem to have calmed down around the Matterhorn. The weather is bad most of the time, and the mountain's slopes are covered in snow. The Italian geologist Felice Giordano is in Zermatt. He collects rocks and sketches the Matterhorn pyramid. To the trained eye, his barometric records and geological study are obviously those of a scientist with alpinist ambitions. When he returns from his ascent of Mont Blanc, which he dared to climb via the Col du Tacul and the Col du Géant, as if he were trying to prove to his Italian colleagues that it was indeed possible to reach the highest summit of the Alps from Courmayeur, he sees the Matterhorn for the first time. "Magnificent," he writes in his diary. "A true, rugged, gloomy, and menacing obelisk." At the Riffelsee, he sketches the Matterhorn and marks the altitude of the shoulder on its southwest ridge. "This is the highest point that has been reached from the other side so far," he writes. "According to my findings, the Carrels and Tyndall reached the base of the beak on the Lion Ridge. It's only another 500 feet [150 meters] to the summit! In order to reach it, you would have to hammer steps into the rock over a stretch of about 100 feet [30 meters]. Three or four stonemasons could do this in eight to ten days for a fee of twenty liras per worker per day." This is Giordano's strategy for an Italian ascent of the Matterhorn.

Crossing the Col de Saint-Théodule on his way to Giomein to visit Jean-Antoine Carrel, Giordano coincidentally meets him on the col. "Carrel is one of the few Valtournenche guides who has the ability to scale the Matterhorn and has spoken with Sella about it," he writes in his diary.

Quintino Sella, geologist, finance minister, and president of the CAI, had summoned Carrel to meet him in the town of Biella. Jean-Antoine returns home with the request—or rather the order—to prepare the ascent of the Matterhorn for Sella and to be available for the expedition of the CAI in the summer of 1865.

Giordano and Carrel meet again in Giomein. "I spent a whole evening with Carrel and Canon Gorret," Giordano writes in his diary. Obviously they discussed the ascent of the Matterhorn. What else?

A few days later, Giordano participates in the congress of the Italian Society for Natural Science and as usual stays at Sella's home. Over a good bottle of Barolo wine the evening's conversation is dominated by the Matterhorn climb. Sella is aware of Tyndall's and Whymper's attempts. However, being a patriot and president of the CAI he does not want to witness the English "snatching the mountain away" from them. As if the Matterhorn would belong to its conquerors in the end. The victory over the Matterhorn has to be an "Italian victory." "Italian alpinism needs such a triumph," Sella writes. "First and foremost, because such a heroic deed would certainly have a role-model effect on the young people of Italy."

Giordano is tasked with preparing and leading this challenging undertaking. In Sella's eyes he is the epitome of an alpinist with modern views, who is not only focused on the ascent but also concerned with scientific goals. Being a minister of a unified Italy, Sella cannot absent himself from Italy to climb during the planned time but is due to follow later.

Now that Tyndall has given up on the Matterhorn, only Whymper and the Carrel and Giordano team are left in the game, and, with Jean-Antoine joining his party, the Piedmontese sees himself at an advantage. Whymper, having repeatedly failed to climb the mountain from Breuil, starts having doubts about Carrel's route on the Italian side. He now wants to reach the summit via a different route. "Are the layered rocks on the east face more favorable?" he wonders. The gradient there also seems less precipitous to him. The east side of the mountain leading up the Hörnli Ridge must be easier. Reaching the top from there must be possible! Michel Croz, the famous Chamonix guide who accompanied Whymper during the difficult first ascent of the Barre des Écrins in the Dauphiné Alps, takes on the challenge and teams up with Whymper.

CHAPTER 16

IN THE MEANTIME, WHYMPER HAS recognized his shortcomings and realizes that he is not an adequate independent climber. He wants to acquire the skills to climb mountains as autonomously as Jean-Antoine Carrel does, to be able to choose the best route and then simply rely on himself. Will he be able to achieve that? His ambition to make first ascents is now fueled by the desire to achieve it without guides. He sets the summers of 1864 and 1865 aside to acquire the necessary skills. Back in London, he reads numerous reports by experienced alpinists and studies their failures in order to avoid making the same mistakes as his predecessors. Success on the mountain is no accident, and human error is often the reason for failure. It is humans who make mistakes, not mountains. Every failure can teach something useful for the next attempt. This is another reason why Whymper has not given up yet.

At 13,524 feet (4,122 meters), the Aiguille Verte rises into the sky like a white pyramid east of Chamonix. Despite the fact that it has been attempted twenty times, its peak is still untouched when Whymper sets his eyes on it.

"No, it has never been climbed," says Croz when they meet in Chamonix.
"Why not?"

"Apparently there have been some failed attempts."

"By inexperienced tourists?"

"Not only those. There were also some guides who abandoned the climb after they came across the first difficulty."

Whymper knows that the Chamonix guides have their tricks to attract rich clients, especially Mont Blanc aspirants seeking prestige. The guides know how to squeeze money out of them. Their fraternity often jokes about it blatantly: "An unclimbed Verte is a better source of income than a climbed one."

For the loner Whymper, on the other hand, the "unclimbed" status poses a compelling challenge. His compatriots of the prestigious Alpine Club have not yet recognized his accomplishments, which could be due to his stubborn character and nonconforming behavior. He turns up at fancy dinners wearing a sweater, not a dinner jacket. "His ambitions are too big, his budget too small," club members gossip. The mountain guides, who Whymper likes to criticize, also view him with skepticism. Why is he only interested in virgin mountains? Why does he want to climb the Aiguille Verte? He is neither a lord nor a professor but only a wood engraver from a simple background. For many he remains an enigma. People know that he travels on behalf of an English publishing house, visits Switzerland and France, and makes wood engravings to illustrate a coffee-table book about the Alps. Doing this, he has become a demanding climber, one with a reputation for changing his guides all too often.

On June 14, 1865, Whymper meets the Grindelwald guide Christian Almer, also called Isegrind. A little later they are joined by Michel Croz, from Le Tour in the Chamonix Valley, as well as Franz Biner. Whymper is excited.

He writes in his journal, "It is not possible to find two leading guides who work together more harmoniously than Croz and Almer. Croz speaks French alone and Almer little else than German. Biner speaks both languages and is useful on that account."

As Whymper speaks reasonable French, a bit of German, as well as the guides' language, known as Alpine English, he is able to communicate adequately about alpine matters. On June 16 the team succeeds in making the first ascent of the Grand Cornier, a mountain of about 13,000 feet (almost 4,000 meters).

On June 20, Whymper climbs the Theodulhorn with Croz. During the climb they have a good view of the Matterhorn and Whymper shows his guide an alternative route for the ascent. "Instead of following the southwest ridge, I would like to access it from the right gully on the south face, then step onto it via the ramps on the right and then go across the Hörnli Ridge to climb diagonally toward the start of the beak." It is a bold plan, one most guides would not take seriously. However, Croz thinks it is possible and agrees.

During the years that Whymper has attempted to climb the Matterhorn, he has developed a love for snowfields, but he is still no fan of ridges. He is also convinced that from Zermatt the Matterhorn looks steeper than it really is. From the Riffelberg or Gornergrat, he writes, the mountain naturally looks more precipitous because its eastern face is viewed more directly.

"Why are there places on this eastern face where the snow remains all year round?" Whymper wants to know.

"The slopes are not steep enough," Croz replies.

"Forty-five degrees at the most," Whymper estimates. "The mountain has a different profile seen from the alpine huts in Staffel. From there it seems almost flat."

"Apparently," says Croz.

"From the slopes between the Zmutt Glacier and the Matterhorn Glacier, the east face can be seen in profile," says Whymper. "I think the angle scarcely exceeds forty degrees."

"The stratified rock on the southwest ridge is less favorable for climbers than the rock on the east side," Whymper says to Croz.

"Definitely," Croz agrees.

"Saussure discovered that the stratified rocks dip to the northeast at an angle of about forty-five degrees."

"Why have you never tried it from the other side?"

"It was only during my failed attempt on the southwest ridge two years ago that I noticed I had always tackled the mountain from the wrong side."

"Is this the reason for your decision to climb the other ridge on the opposite side?"

"Yes, because it's easier to climb."

Whymper will later write in *Scrambles Amongst the Alps*, "A more serious hindrance to mounting the south-west ridge is found in the dip of its rocks to the west-south-west . . . the rocks on some portions of the ridge leading from the Col du Lion to the summit dip outward, and that fractured edges overhang . . . It will be readily understood that such an arrangement is not favorable for climbers."

Whymper is convinced that he now holds the key to the first ascent of the Matterhorn. If the eastern face were a 4,000-foot (1,200-meter) natural staircase, the mountain would have been climbed a long time ago. Fresh snow usually brings out long terraced lines up on the mountain, lines that are roughly parallel to each other, but that does not make the ridge a staircase.

After Croz has agreed, Whymper approaches the guides Almer and Biner, proposing the route from the Matterhorn Glacier to the northeast ridge via the gully: "We ascend the gully to its head, cross over the southeast ridge onto the eastern face, then diagonally climb the snow slope, with the view of arriving at the snow on the northeast ridge. The remainder of the ascent is to be made by the broken rocks on the north side of the mountain."

All three of them listen carefully to Whymper's route description. They nod in unison.

"The strategy is good," one of them says.

The party descends to Breuil, where they engage Luc Meynet as tent porter. Whymper intends to take three days for the ascent.

"We'll establish the first bivouac on the rocks at the top of the gully."

"Agreed," Croz says.

"On the second day we attack the summit and return to the tent."

"Too much," Almer observes.

"On the third day, we come back to Breuil."

Favre's kitchen is soon in commotion, preparing rations for three days.

On June 21, 1865, the five men head toward the pass called Breuiljoch (or Col du Breuil). When they are in full view of the gully they turn left at a right angle. The closer they approach now, the more favorable it looks. There is a good deal of snow. Under the cover of the cliffs they proceed up the right edge of the snow gully. Whymper describes it in *Scrambles Amongst the Alps* as "sometimes cutting steps into the snow and sometimes mounting the rocks." While the guides take a rest, Whymper goes to a little promontory to examine their proposed route more closely and to admire the couloir that leads straight up into the heart of the mountain for a full 1,000 feet (300 meters). He sees a few small stones skidding down through the curved groove in the middle of the gully, too far off to hit him. But then some cupboard-sized boulders start tumbling down.

"Rockfall!" he cries out.

At first the guides, who are busy eating and chatting, are oblivious, but now they dash in all directions, seeking protection under overhanging rocks. Countless boulders from the wall 800 feet (250 meters) above them come whizzing past before they crash into the rock lower down. The rocks crack, ricochet, and cover a hundred feet or more in a bound.

Whymper's words: "Mutton legs are pitched aside, a wineskin is dropped, its contents gushing out, and the men cower under overhangs, trying to make themselves as small as possible. It is the beginning of yet another failure."

"We must go back," Almer calls out when the rockfall ends.

"Retreat?" Whymper asks. He suggests they first have a look at the rocks above them.

"Impossible," Croz says.

But Whymper starts to clamber up higher. He does not want to go down without having at least tried. After a few minutes he is brought to a halt.

"Too dangerous," he thinks.

Almer, a hundred feet below, shakes his head. Biner is out of sight. Croz keeps an eye on Whymper—and on Meynet, who is following him.

"It's useless!" Croz shouts up to Whymper.

"You're right," he acknowledges to himself, his teeth grinding.

Once again Whymper has failed. At his direction they make a straight track for the Col du Breuil to attack the summit again from the east side. The twenty-five-year-old Whymper is determined and pursues his goal like a lunatic, but again he is faced with obstacles. Dark clouds are gathering from the south, and a strong wind is blowing, but he is not willing to give up, even though his guides have lost all hope.

"Why don't you try to climb a mountain that can be climbed?" Almer asks.

Whymper nods, disappointed, but he cannot share this attitude.

"Why don't you understand? The Matterhorn is not climbable," says Biner.

"Only if we don't try," Whymper replies.

"I'll climb any mountain with you but the Matterhorn!" Almer says.

"Just one more try," Whymper pleads.

"If we cross over to the other side we'll lose three days," Croz says.

Whymper knows it but doesn't say another word.

"We won't succeed," Croz adds. He is sure Whymper will eventually understand.

"Impossible. Completely and utterly impossible!" Biner calls out.

"Were you not intending to make ascents in the Mont Blanc range?" Croz says, trying to lure him. "I think they can be made."

"You don't understand. I want to make the impossible possible—the Matterhorn."

"But I have to be in Chamonix on the twenty-seventh," says Croz. "I have an engagement."

Whymper hesitates. He trusts Croz and needs his strong arms.

When it begins snowing, they descend in silence.

They go directly to Breuil and then on to Valtournenche, where they stay the night. The next day, they head for the Mont Blanc range via Châtillon and then up the Aosta Valley to Courmayeur.

On June 24, the party succeeds in ascending the Grand Jorasses from Courmayeur, almost without incident. Back in Chamonix, Whymper and Croz part due to the guide's commitment with another client.

On June 29, Whymper, together with Almer and Biner, makes the first ascent of the Aiguille Verte. After their feat, the trio traverses the Mont Blanc range from Montenvers, reaches Courmayeur, and continues to Aosta via the sunken ridge of the Glacier de Talèfre, which has never been climbed.

"This guy is indestructible," the guides think. He just won't stop! The trio has climbed almost 100,000 feet (30,000 meters) in altitude in the past few weeks. Whymper is in great shape. He longs to go back to the Matterhorn—now or never! Almer and Biner have had enough, though. They are done with the Matterhorn.

Back in Breuil, Whymper pays Jean-Antoine Carrel a visit. Even though the rivalry between the two men has increased, they are still the ideal rope team. More than anything, Whymper marvels at Carrel's extraordinary abilities on the mountain. He senses his own awkwardness and sees Carrel's sure-footed moves as being "almost more like those of a chamois."

In the next few days, the two reach the top of the Gran Tournalin above the village of Valtournenche and climb almost 6,500 feet (2,000 meters) in less than four hours. Are they trying to prove who has more stamina? Are they testing themselves?

CHAPTER 17

THE LETTER WAS SENT FROM Turin and dated July 7, 1865.

Dear Quintino! I am starting off heavily armed for the
destination you wrote of. I have the best equipment. Two
days ago, I sent the first tent, 300 meters of rope, some
iron hoops and rings, provisions for ourselves, [and] a
spirit stove to [heat] water and tea. Altogether it weighs
about 100 kilos. I have also sent Carrel 22 liras to meet
these articles in Châtillon and transport them to Valtournenche and Breuil at once. I shall be there myself
tomorrow evening to superintend the work. I am taking with me a second tent, three barometers, your own
among them, and the *Annuaire du Bureau des Longitudes*.
As soon as I reach the scene of operations, I will write
to you again. You need only trouble about your own
personal requirements, which means you will need your
headgear, two or three rugs and some good cigars. If
possible, please bring some good wine and a few shekels

because I have only been able to bring about 300 liras with me. Let us, then, set out to attack this Devil's mountain, and let us see that we succeed, if only Whymper has not been there beforehand.

Felice Giordano has meticulously prepared the Italian expedition. He has tested the strength of the ropes and bought tents. On July 8, in Valtournenche, he meets Jean-Antoine Carrel who has just come back from a reconnaissance tour of the Matterhorn with César Carrel, Charles Gorret, and Jean-Joseph Maquignaz during which they were forced to retreat due to bad weather.

Before he left, Jean-Antoine had spoken to Whymper and offered to accompany him on his attempt on the Swiss side of the Matterhorn. Carrel promised Whymper to be available until Tuesday, July 11—provided the weather improved. As it does not improve on the arranged day, there is no point in trying. The Englishman knows as well as Carrel that the Matterhorn cannot be scaled in bad weather. For this reason, Carrel feels free to commit to Sella and Giordano without breaking his word. He is required to cut steps into the Matterhorn for an easy ascent.

When Whymper descends to Valtournenche on Monday, July 10, a climbing party moves toward him. To his surprise, he sees that it is Carrel accompanying a man unknown to him. Both carry heavy loads. Carrel informs Whymper that he will not be able to serve him after Wednesday, July 12, as he has some prior engagements.

"What engagements?" Whymper wants to know.

"A family of distinction."

"Why didn't you say this before?"

"Because it wasn't settled."

"I asked you first."

"No, the engagement is of long standing, long before you even arrived in Valtournenche."

"We depart tomorrow morning," Whymper asserts.

"Unfortunately, the weather will be bad."

Whymper is now without a guide. In the evening, he and Carrel meet at the inn and recount their adventures over a glass of wine like old friends.

But Carrel does not tell Whymper that he will be tackling the mountain with Giordano.

It is now July 11. The guides, including Jean-Antoine Carrel, head out at the crack of dawn. The Italian expedition has commenced. The team has set out to pave the way to the summit for Quintino Sella and the Kingdom of Italy: "Viva l'Italia!"

Whymper, who still thinks that he has a claim on Carrel, is very angry. Is the Italians' pay better? Did Carrel favor the Italians over him, his protégé, for money? His outrage is not surprising, but he knows it is not really a betrayal. He cannot criticize Carrel and his men for not giving away Giordano's plans. It is not fair to accuse the Italians of cheating; after all, Carrel kept his promise. He would have set out with Whymper on their arranged attempt had the weather not been bad.

At this point, Giordano has not learned of Carrel's passion, his obsession to climb the Matterhorn. To Giordano, Carrel's only duty is to prepare the way to the summit for him and Sella. With this belief, he spends the next few days casually awaiting Carrel's confirmation that the ascent route has been prepared.

In the Breuil Inn on the eve of July 11, at the foot of the Col de Saint-Théodule, Giordano again writes to Sella.

Dear Quintino!
It's about time I wrote to you. I reached Valtournenche on the afternoon of Saturday, July 8. There I found Carrel, who had just returned from a reconnaissance expedition on the Matterhorn, which he had to cut short due to bad weather. Whymper had arrived two or three days before me. He wanted to set off immediately and engaged Carrel, who had not yet received my letters. Fortunately, the weather turned bad. Whymper was unable to make his attempt. Carrel, who was only committed to Whymper for a few days, left him and came with me, with five other men. All selected by Carrel, the best guides of the valley among them: César Carrel, the son of Jean-Jacques,

Charles Gorret, the brother of Abbé Gorret, and Jean-Joseph Maquignaz, a stonemason.

Our expedition is going ahead with Carrel as the leader. In order to avoid attention, we shifted food provisions, ropes, and other equipment to a remote hut in Avouil, which will serve as our headquarters.

Four of the six men will climb up slowly and prepare the route, two porters will carry the equipment, and I will remain in Breuil for the time being.

The weather, the god we all fear and on whom all will depend, has been hitherto very changeable and rather cruel. Yesterday morning it was snowing on the Matterhorn, but the skies cleared in the evening.

In the night from July 10 to 11, the men left with the tents. I hope that they have reached a great height. Unfortunately, the weather is turning misty again and the Matterhorn is still covered. I hope the mists will soon disperse. Weather permitting, I hope in three or four days to know how I stand. It all depends on the weather.

Carrel is extremely cautious, even suspicious toward me. He told me not to come up until he should send me word. He wishes personally to make sure of the last bits. As seen from here they do not seem to me to be absolutely inaccessible, but before saying that one must try them; and it is also necessary to ascertain whether we can bivouac at a point much higher than Whymper's highest. As soon as I have any good news I will send a message to St. Vincent, the nearest telegraph office, with a telegram containing a few words. Once you receive it, please come at once!

Meanwhile, on receipt of the present, please send me a few lines in reply with some advice, because I am up to the ears in difficulty here, what with the weather, the expense, and Whymper. I have tried to keep everything secret, but that fellow whose life seems to depend on the Matterhorn is here, suspiciously prying into everything.

Just in case, I have taken all competent men away from him, yet he is so enamored of this mountain that he may go up with others and make a scene. He is here in this hotel, and I try to avoid speaking to him. In short: I will do my best to succeed, and I have hopes, provided Aeolus be on our side!

I will write no more at present, hoping soon to send you a favorable sign. I trust this news from the Alps will refresh you somewhat in the heat of Turin and the oppression of ministerial affairs.

Minister Sella is preoccupied with financial operations these days, and his workload is exacerbated by the fact that the capital of the Kingdom of Italy is being moved from Turin to Florence. It is not the expense of the mountaineering expedition that worries him, it is that politics do not leave him any time for the mountains. How can a minister quickly race up the Matterhorn in between meetings?

While Whymper meticulously follows Carrel's progress on the mountain through his binoculars, Giordano already feels victorious. He spends his time waiting and going on excursions, sometimes accompanied by Amé Gorret, the young vicar of Cogne. They discuss various topics, cross the Col de Saint-Théodule together, and climb a few surrounding peaks. On these outings Giordano sketches and takes barometric measurements, and in between he points his binoculars toward the Matterhorn. Again and again!

Whymper, on the other hand, feels paralyzed without Carrel, but he has not given up his goal. The climbing aids Carrel is currently installing could also be of use to him to reach the summit. Whymper even sees his advantage in the bad weather as it will bring Carrel's expedition to a halt.

Suddenly Whymper springs into action and packs up his belongings. "Is he going to Zermatt?" Giordano wonders. "To reach the summit from the other side? Before the Italians reach it?" After all, the northeast ridge is Whymper's final trump card.

CHAPTER 18

On July 11, Whymper stands by the door of the inn looking through his telescope. He observes a team of climbers near the high pastures moving toward the Matterhorn.

"What is happening?" he excitedly asks Favre, the landlord, who stands next to him.

"An Italian expedition is trying to climb the Matterhorn."

"Who is the leader of this party?"

"Carrel."

"Jean-Antoine?"

"Yes. Jean-Antoine Carrel."

"Is César there too?"

"Yes."

Whymper realizes that the Italian party's ascent must have been planned for a long time. Carrel's attempt on July 6 was a preliminary reconnaissance, and the mule that was carrying provisions up the mountain was conveying stores for the attack.

"These men will get nowhere," Whymper rants.

"Why not?"

"The guides from Valtournenche work like the Swiss guides—only for money and not for honor."

"The noble man behind them is Signor Giordano," Favre whispers. "Apparently he has been ordered to find a way to the summit and have it prepared for Minister Sella. With ladders, steps, and fixed ropes." Favre's pleasure over Whymper's discomfiture can be heard in every word.

Whymper retires to his room, smokes a cigar, and ponders how he can possibly outmaneuver the Italians. A mule load of provisions means extra weight and loss of time. He needs to act quickly now. Whymper sends messengers in all directions. He looks for porters for his baggage, but not a single porter can be found. The ablest men are on the mountain; there is not a single mule herder in Breuil. Meynet is engaged in some important cheese-making operation. Fortunately, fog is still engulfing the mountain.

They will need at least a week to reach the top, Whymper calculates. This leaves him enough time to shift to Zermatt and attempt the mountain from the east. "If my route is as good as I think it is, I'll reach the summit in three days. If not, I'll be back in Breuil before the Italians' summit attempt," he thinks. It is all about outwitting the outwitters.

Around noon Whymper sees a roped party just below the Col de Saint-Théodule coming from Zermatt. A young Englishman with one of Peter Taugwalder's sons, as he later finds out when the man returns to Breuil.

"I am Francis Douglas, brother of the Marquis of Queensberry," the man introduces himself.

"You have climbed the Obergabelhorn, haven't you?" Whymper asks.

"Yes."

"Congratulations."

"Thanks."

"What's next?"

"I am going back to Zermatt tomorrow."

"May I engage your porter?" Whymper asks briskly.

"No problem. I don't have any baggage."

"Is he not the son of the famous Peter Taugwalder?"

"Yes, the second eldest."

"I've heard about him."

"Old Peter has suggested something to me."

"Yes?" Whymper asks excitedly. "News from the Matterhorn?"

"Peter Taugwalder has discovered an ascent route on the Hörnli Ridge."

"Does he really think it possible to climb the Matterhorn from the Swiss side?"

"Yes, he does."

"Is this why you are here, Lord Douglas?"

"Yes."

Before long the two men know that they will team up and tackle the mountain together. Favre lends them one of his men, and, heavily laden, they climb across the Col de Saint-Théodule and the Furggengletscher to the little chapel at the Schwarzsee, where they deposit Whymper's equipment—tent, blankets, and ropes. He has brought 550 feet (160 meters) of rope: two lengths of a stout Manila rope—one 200 feet (60 meters) and the other 150 feet—and 200 feet of a lighter, weaker rope.

Whymper senses that the route on the Hörnli Ridge is his last chance. Just like old Peter, he is sure that the east face looks worse than it actually is. The ridge only gets properly steep above the shoulder. But does it get too steep?

CHAPTER 19

ON THE MORNING OF JULY 12, Giordano walks up to the hut in Avouil and finds that two of Carrel's men came down to fetch provisions the previous night. They apparently returned to the mountain immediately. The Avouil herdsmen say that Carrel had reached to below the shoulder to pitch the last tent as high as possible.

The following day, Giordano looks through his binoculars from Giomein and is shocked, even shattered, by what he sees: huge icicles have formed on the mountain. Carrel will not be able to get anything done in these conditions. Meanwhile Whymper is on his way and might already be high up on the other side of the mountain.

But Carrel and his people continue to climb, and it is Luc Meynet who spots them. "They are working below the top of the shoulder."

The evening is magnificent: the air is soft, the contours of the mountain are sharp, the sky is filled with stars. Giordano hopes that Carrel will send someone to fetch him. He wants to be part of the conquest of the Matterhorn. That night he doesn't sleep much. He is convinced that they will call for him—for the summit!

Nobody on the Italian side of the Matterhorn knows that Whymper has already started his summit attack on the Hörnli Ridge.

On July 14, in the evening, Giordano writes to Sella:

> Breuil Inn on July 14, 1865
> Dear Quintino!
> I have sent Abbé Gorret with a dispatch to St. Vincent, seven hours' walk from here. But to make sure you will get this news, I am writing this letter as well.
>
> Something significant has happened! Today at two o'clock in the afternoon, I saw Carrel and his team at the highest point [yet reached] of the Matterhorn. Many others saw them too. Success is almost certain, even though two days ago the weather was still unfavorable and the mountain was covered in snow.
>
> If you possibly can, please come here as quickly as possible or send a telegraph to St. Vincent stating your plans. I don't even know whether you are in Turin! I haven't had any news from there for eight days; that's why I am writing to you unprepared. If you are not here tomorrow or [don't] send a telegraph, I will go up myself and fly our flag from the summit. It is important for our cause. I will do my utmost to wait for your arrival.
>
> Whymper is attacking the summit from the other side I believe, and I hope, in vain.

Giordano feels proud, excited, and in awe. At the same time, he is impatient—and disconcerted that Carrel has not come to get him for the summit attack. Does Carrel want all the glory for himself?

CHAPTER 20

ON THE EVENING OF JULY 12, Lord Douglas arrives in Zermatt and visits old Peter Taugwalder. They sit in the hotel's common room, and Douglas explains the situation: "Carrel is on the other side of the mountain together with some guides from Valtournenche. High up! At the moment they are being stopped by thick clouds and snow, which will postpone their ascent a bit. We might be able to outmaneuver the Italians."

"Maybe," Taugwalder says. "In any case, it will require two guides." At that moment, Whymper walks in. He had waited in front of the big dark wooden house on the church square where Taugwalder lives with his family.

"The gentlemen know each other?" Taugwalder asks.

"Yes, we want to climb the Matterhorn together," Douglas says.

"With me as the only guide?" Taugwalder asks. "Impossible!"

"I don't need a guide," Whymper responds.

"It's difficult," Taugwalder says. "If there is one guest without a guide, I will still be responsible for him."

"I am confident enough to climb on my own—"

"Not when I am responsible," Taugwalder interrupts. Then he turns to Douglas and asks doubtfully: "Is this man any good as a guide?"

"We are both independent climbers," Douglas assures him. "We may not be mountain guides, but what difference does it make?"

"And who will make the decisions on the mountain?" Taugwalder wants to know.

"You and me," says Whymper.`

"In the hotels, the gentlemen give orders. In the mountains, it's the guides," Taugwalder asserts.

"I want to have a say on the mountain," Whymper responds.

"The guide guides. He bears the responsibility, which means he also makes the decisions."

Taugwalder knows that Whymper has a big mouth, but he also knows that he can climb. However, he is not prepared for the Englishman, twenty years his junior, to treat him like a servant.

"You should look for a guide for yourself," Taugwalder sums up.

"Peter is a great decision-maker," Douglas says calmingly. "A first-class mountain guide."

"I know," Whymper replies in order to restore peace.

At this hour, another Matterhorn aspirant arrives at the Hotel Monte Rosa. Monsieur and Madame Seiler welcome their new guest, Reverend Charles Hudson, in the hotel lobby. They have known Hudson for eleven years, since Hudson's first ascent of the Durfourspitze (Dufour Peak). They feel very grateful toward the vicar as he has recommended the hotel to many foreign visitors.

Hudson books two rooms, one for himself and one for his young companion, Mr. Hadow, and passes on some regards: "Unfortunately Mr. Kennedy had to go back to England for business," he says of his friend who failed on the Matterhorn in January 1862.

Shortly afterward, Hudson and Hadow climb up the little hill right behind the hotel and continue on to a sheep pasture from where they have a magnificent view of the Matterhorn. Just a quick excursion before dinner.

Whymper, now also on his way to the Hotel Monte Rosa, sees a familiar face among the mountain guides sitting on the wall waiting for clients. It's Croz!

"You are the last person I expected to see in Zermatt," Whymper says.

"I've waited for Mr. Birkbeck for a long time in Chamonix but in vain."

"What happened?"

"He had to return to England due to his illness."

"What happened then?"

"Mr. Kennedy, who hired me afterward, also had to go back to Leeds."

"And now?" Whymper asks excitedly.

"I am here with Hudson. He and his companion, Mr. Hadow, are up there to take a look at the Matterhorn. They want to study the Hörnli Ridge," Croz says a little bit sheepishly.

"I thought you were done with the Matterhorn!"

Croz tries to hide his discomfiture.

"Maybe."

"Shall we tackle the mountain together, now that we are both convinced it can be climbed?"

Croz gives him a look.

"So?" Whymper asks.

"I've been hired by Hudson."

"Does everyone want to climb this mountain all of a sudden?"

Hudson is also surprised when he learns that Whymper—the man who stole the first ascent of the Aguille de Verte from him—is in Zermatt. Him, of all people! Hudson looks at the Matterhorn from his hotel window, just as the evening sunlight touches its north face. The northwest ridge to its right is now a silhouette and looks like a sharp razor blade. "I wonder where the Italians are?" he asks himself. "When Whymper and Douglas set out to climb the Hörnli Ridge with old Peter tomorrow morning, I'll be left out in the cold again," he thinks.

In the evening, they all meet in the dining room of the Hotel Monte Rosa: Lord Douglas, Reverend Hudson, Hadow, and Whymper. They all have the same goal, but they have no common strategy. They all would prefer to set out individually with their respective guides: Douglas with Taugwalder, and Hudson and Hadow with Croz. Only Whymper does not have a guide. After having dismissed Almer and Biner, and Carrel having deserted him, he is on his own. There is Peter Perren, though. If he could only get him here with a magic wand! Perren has repeatedly said that he would like to be part of the first ascent of the Matterhorn.

"Peter Perren is climbing Monte Rosa with tourists," Seiler says.

"Why don't we all join together?" Whymper dares to suggest.

Had none of them thought of that possibility? No sooner is the idea broached then they have agreed and decided to set out together the next morning.

"Hurrah, let's climb the Matterhorn!"

"Do you think Hadow is strong enough?" Whymper asks Hudson out of Hadow's earshot.

"Why wouldn't he be?" Hudson replies.

"What has he climbed in the Alps?"

"Mr. Hadow has climbed Mont Blanc in less time than most men," Hudson says.

"What else?"

"A few similar ascents."

"On rock?"

"Little rock."

"Enough experience?"

"We can take him."

"For sure?"

"Sure!"

So Hadow will come along. Now only one question remains. Will Croz and old Peter suffice as guides? All four Englishmen think so, for Whymper, Douglas, and Hudson consider themselves experienced mountaineers.

"Croz and Taugwalder shall decide themselves whether we should engage porters," Whymper says, "and, if so, how many."

"Agreed," Taugwalder says a little later.

The decision made in the dining room of the Hotel Monte Rosa on the evening of July 12, 1865, is witnessed by hotel proprietor Seiler. There will be a joint departure for the first ascent of the Matterhorn with two guides and two of Taugwalder's sons to porter equipment to the base of the mountain.

On July 13, the team retrieves the ropes from the chapel at the Schwarz-see. Croz and young Peter Taugwalder, who is to be promoted to guide status soon, go on to have a look at the east face. They pass the night at the base of the Matterhorn. On July 14, just before daybreak, the seven men climb up the face, rapidly moving toward the summit.

CHAPTER 21

IT IS NOON ON JULY 14, 1865. Raspberries from the mountains are being served in the dining room of the Hotel Monte Rosa when Monsieur Seiler steps into the hall and announces: "Gentlemen, the climbers have reached the shoulder of the Matterhorn. We can see them!" The guests quickly hurry outside and gaze up toward the summit, but they cannot see the climbers. Only one of the mountain guides says he can see tiny black dots moving along the snowfield on the shoulder.

On the mountain, when the party turns to the right and crosses over to the northern side, they reach the crux. Here Croz takes the lead. Whymper goes next, followed by Douglas, one of Taugwalder's sons, and Hudson. Hadow and old Peter are at the tail end. Taugwalder's other son left the group after they had set up their bivouac and is already back in Zermatt.

"We have just climbed the most difficult part," Croz says when they reach the snowfield. Whymper needed Croz's assistance to get over a difficult section but now he is certain.

"The Matterhorn is ours!" he calls out. Nothing but 200 feet (60 meters) of easy snow remains to be climbed.

Whymper thinks about the Italians, who started from Breuil four days earlier. Have they already been to the top? Worried that the Italians might beat them at the last moment, he hurries on, and so does Croz. The slope eases off the higher they go. For the final spurt Croz detaches himself from the rope and so does Whymper (by cutting the rope leading to Douglas). Their race ends in a virtual tie atop the Matterhorn's summit.

"No footprints up here!" calls Whymper, who is about a second ahead of Croz.

The summit of the Matterhorn is a ridge about 350 feet (100 meters) long. Could the highest point be on the other end? Even though the northern end of the ridge where they are seems higher than the southern end, Whymper hastens over there effortlessly. With his legs spread and a piece of rope tied around his chest, he reaches the Italian summit and looks across the vast high valley of Breuil. He feels elation.

The sky is completely clear, there is no mist in the valleys, and the surrounding mountains show sharp contours. It sinks in for Whymper: he is the first! Everything seems so close: 8,000 feet (2,400 meters) below he sees blue smoke rising from the chalets, and black forests, meadows, waterfalls, and lakes.

"Hurrah! Hurrah! Hurrah!" Whymper calls out. Again: "Hurrah!"

"Where are our opponents?" Croz wants to know.

Whymper leans over a cliff to peer down the mountain. Far down below on a ridge to the south—he is not mistaken—he can see another climbing team.

"The Italians are down there!" he shouts. Whymper clearly recognizes Jean-Antoine Carrel. Up go Whymper's arms and his hat.

"Croz! Croz! Come over here!"

"Where are they?"

"Down there." Whymper points down to the southern shoulder.

"They are a long way down," Croz observes.

"Croz, we must make them hear us."

Both men yell as loud as they can—and the Italians stop and look up.

"They can hear us!"

Whymper waves to Carrel. Nonchalantly, Croz pushes a boulder down into the abyss. Whymper does the same. The Italians scamper and look for cover.

Then Whymper and Croz walk back to the northern end of the ridge, where the others in their team are now waiting.

"The flagpole," Croz says, and plants a tent pole firmly in the snow.

"But where is the flag?"

"Here it is," Croz answers, pulling off his shirt and attaching it to the pole. But there is not a breath of wind to make it unfurl.

"Hurrah! Victory is ours!" people mistakenly shout in Breuil.

"Hurrah! It's our people up there!" shout people in front of the Hotel Monte Rosa in Zermatt. At 1:30 p.m., just before Whymper and Croz reached the summit, a sharp-eyed guide in Zermatt could see the shape of a person on the summit ridge, with a second and third person following.

In the valleys on both sides of the Matterhorn people are slowly beginning to see the tiny dots on the summit. They are visible from Zermatt and from Valtournenche.

"Seven!" Some of the guests of the Seiler Hotel count out loud.

"They all got up safely!" Seiler says, filled with pride. The dots on the summit disappear briefly and reappear. The hotel guests go back into the dining room. Only Joseph Taugwalder stays on the street and follows his father and elder brother with his binoculars until they start their descent. After a while, he sees a puff of white moving just below them.

"Father, an avalanche!" he cries out—as if old Peter could hear him.

Seiler runs back into the street. Both look up to the north face anxiously, but it is now completely shaded, and they are unable to make out anything.

"This often happens on hot summer days," Seiler says.

"The conquerors of the Matterhorn are now descending," Seiler announces back in the hotel.

CHAPTER 22

THE LETTER, WRITTEN BY Giordano in Breiul, is dated July 15, 1865:

Dear Quintino!

Yesterday was a bad day. It was not our people who reached the summit first, but the English! Whymper, after all, gained the victory over the unfortunate Carrel. As I have already told you, Whymper was desperate and, seeing Carrel climb the mountain, tried his luck on the Zermatt side. Everyone here, and Carrel above all, considered the ascent absolutely impossible on that side, so we were all easy in our minds. On the 11th Carrel was at work on the mountain and pitched his tent at a certain height. On the night between the 11th and 12th, and all of the 12th the weather was horrible, and it snowed on the Matterhorn. On the 13th the weather was fair, and yesterday the 14th it was excellent. On the 13th little work was done, and yesterday Carrel could have reached the summit! He was perhaps only about 500 or 600 feet below, when suddenly at about two p.m., he saw Whymper and six other men standing on the summit. Completely unexpected!

Whymper must have promised a considerable sum to various Swiss guides to take him up, and having been favored with an exceptionally fine day, he succeeded. I had, it is true, sent Carrel word of Whymper's proposed attempt and had enjoined him to get up at any cost, without loss of time to prepare the way, but my warning did not reach him in time. Moreover, Carrel did not believe the ascent from the north to be possible. However, yesterday, as I saw some men on the Matterhorn, and was assured by everyone that they were our party, I sent off the telegram to you, bidding you to come up. But now it's too late!

Poor Carrel. When he saw that he had been forestalled, he did have not the courage to proceed and retreated with all his equipment and baggage. He arrived here late this morning, subdued and tired but not angry. It was then that I sent off another telegram by express to stop you from coming. As you see, even though every man did his duty, it is a lost battle, and I am in great grief.

I think, however, that we can play a counterstroke by someone making the ascent at once on this side, thus proving at any rate that the ascent is feasible this way; Carrel still thinks it possible. I was only vexed with him for bringing down the tents, the ropes, and all the other things that had been carried up with so much labor to a point so near the summit. He puts the blame on the party, who had completely lost heart, and on his fear that I should be unwilling to go to any further expense to reach the summit after Whymper.

At any rate, in order not to return ridiculed as well as unsuccessful, I think that we ought at least to plant our flag on the summit. I at once tried to organize a fresh expedition, but hitherto, with the exception of Carrel and another, I have not found any men of courage I can trust. Some others might, perhaps, be found if I paid them extravagantly, but I do not think it wise to go to such expense; and if their courage is deficient, there will be no certainty of success.

I am therefore trying to fit out the expedition cheaply and will only give up if this one is unsuccessful. Now I shall not even have the satisfaction of going up myself, because Carrel says that, for the sake of quickness and in order to make the best of the short time we have at our disposal, it will be better that they should not have any tourists with them. We must also remember that we are threatened by the weather, which is doubtful. Just see how annoying it all is!

Yesterday was a day of joy in the Tournenche Valley, today is a day of mourning. Yesterday the valley was filled with jubilant cheers as everyone was convinced it was our people who won; today it is filled with disappointment. Poor Carrel is to be pitied, the more so as part of the delay was due to his idea that Whymper would not be able to ascend from Zermatt. I am trying to act like Terentius Varro after the battle of Cannae.

PS—Notwithstanding what has happened, you might still make the first ascent from the Italian side, if you had the time. But till now Carrel has not assured me that the way is feasible right to the top. That is why I have not telegraphed you again; perhaps I shall come to Turin myself in a couple of days.

The locals of Breuil have now, like Giordano, realized that the dots they saw from their side of the Matterhorn were Whymper's people and not theirs. At the moment there is no more news about the ascent, only that Carrel and his group were on the shoulder, not far from Tyndall's cairn, when they heard Whymper's and Croz's victorious shouts. When Croz spotted the Italians below them, he had exclaimed: "Ah! *Les coquins* [the rascals] are down there!" This was followed by a loud rumble of rocks, which Croz is said to have thrown down the mountain to attract the Italians' attention. When Carrel looked up, he recognized Whymper's white trousers.

Carrel later says that the reason for his retreat on July 14, the day of England's victory, was not Whymper having reached the summit but his people being hesitant. They felt unsafe. Carrel and Maquinaz had wanted to proceed, but the others did not now see the point in continuing. And as

Carrel wanted to get everyone back down to the valley safely, they retreated. Whymper views the situation differently: Carrel retreated as a loser and left the mountain in a hurry.

The people of Valtournenche also view Carrel's retreat as surrender. Behind closed doors, they comment, discuss, and ridicule. The fact that he has never experienced an accident during all his attempts at the Matterhorn does not seem to matter. Only Giordano objects. But he is also met with ridicule, even though he was not there, for Carrel had no confidence in his ability to reach the summit.

"How could Carrel, who everyone follows blindly, possibly give up so close to the summit?" his countrymen wonder. Did he lose courage when he saw Whymper on the top? Or was he never in a position to actually scale the Matterhorn?

No matter how honorable it would have been to carry on and reach the top a few hours after his rival, Carrel never risks too much. As if care and responsibility for his people were in his genes. His dream was to be the first to reach the summit of his mountain, nothing less. It is too late now. Honor belongs to those who deserve it. The Englishman's obsession was stronger than his own, and luck was on Whymper's side.

For the time being, Carrel is not interested in a second ascent. He has dedicated almost ten years of his life to make the first ascent, and he feels little commitment to Sella and Giordano, who would like to boost Italian patriotism with a trivial silver medal, a second ascent (albeit a first ascent from the Italian side). Carrel may be a patriot, but like Whymper he is not one to fly a national flag from the summit.

One reason Carrel is not enthusiastic about now making the first ascent from the Italian side is that he does not want to present the Matterhorn on a plate to Giordano and Sella. He is not interested in this kind of service. The question of whether his route is more strenuous than the English route is not his concern either. All he thinks about is that the first ascent has been taken away from him.

"How could Carrel have forgotten his duty?" some are musing.

"Which duty?"

"To conquer the Matterhorn for Italy!"

Carrel will never respond to this.

CHAPTER 23

Disheartened, Jean-Antoine Carrel hides out in his hut in Avouil the day after his return from the mountain.

On the following day, July 15, he visits Giordano, who soon afterward writes in his diary, "An evil day. Early in the morning Carrel, more dead than alive, came to tell me he had been forestalled. He had reckoned on climbing to the top today, and expected to be able to force a passage not by the highest tower, which he considers impossible, but on the Zmutt side, where the snow is. [But] he capitulated after Whymper's victory. I have insisted that he and the others shall at least try and ascend and plant our flag."

Giordano tries everything to turn the Italian defeat into an Italian victory. Still unsure whether the last rock wall below the summit can be circumvented, Carrel hesitates, but in the end it is his men who refuse to make another attempt.

"I have invested a lot of time and money to be the first on the summit," Giordano tells the guides.

Nobody responds.

"Our initial goal is lost, but this is also about you, about the honor and interests of the Valtournenche guides."

Their answer remains no. Then Amé Gorret, the vicar, comes forward and offers to accompany Jean-Antoine, determined to help him get to the top. Only this proposal makes Carrel feel obliged to make another attempt. Eight years earlier, he and Gorret had failed to climb the Matterhorn together, but now they team up again to finish what they started. Two of Favre's servants—Jean-Augustin Meynet and Jean-Baptiste Bich—as well as two porters will fill out the expedition. Giordano wants to go with them at all cost, but Carrel vehemently refuses to take him.

"A tourist," he says, "is an additional risk for the success and survival of my people."

"I can help you carry," Giordano says, almost pleading.

"Making sure that everyone survives is a burden nobody can take away from me."

"I can take some of that burden."

"No, the responsibility is solely mine."

Giordano asks Carrel to give this to him in writing, saying he might need some proof later to save his honor. Carrel refuses.

"A nasty feverish night during which I lived through all bitterness of disappointment. I only made one barometric observation," Giordano writes in his diary the following morning.

It is Sunday, July 16, 1865. It seems like a conspiracy when the residents of Breuil flock into their small church for early Mass. Carrel and his group leave for the mountain after the service. Giordano is left behind in Giomein.

"I have once more made the great sacrifice of waiting at the foot of the peak instead of climbing it," he writes in another letter to Sella. "Carrel still snubs me. I assure you that this is the most painful thing I have ever endured in my life."

At 2:00 p.m. Carrel and his team reach the bivouac at the base of the Great Tower. Amé Gorret is especially enthusiastic. What a view!

The following morning, they reach Tyndall's cairn on the shoulder. Gorret suggests ascending by the ridge and scaling the last tower straight up.

"This is insane," says Carrel, who is certainly in a much better position to assess the terrain than the vicar. "Only if we traverse to the west of the peak and go up on the Zmutt side will we stand a chance."

"You are in charge."

When they traverse over to the left across a steep band, icicles fall down from above.

"Careful!" Carrel yells.

Too late. Gorret's arm has been hit. Carrel hesitates, but only briefly. Would it be better to use the direct line after all? Without ladders or wooden sticks?

"Impossible," he tells himself.

The way back to the Breuil ridge is difficult and probably the most dangerous section of the whole climb. Is there an alternative? Carrel looks up. Can he see the face of a monster cut in the rock a hundred feet above him? Is that an ape's face skeptically looking down on him? To the right of the ape's nose he identifies a possible ascent route. "Climb the overhang into the right eye socket, continue left, and gain the summit via the left eyebrow," he tells himself. It would be a possible route if only it were not so steep.

High up in the clouds he sees dark long hair with blond streaks. Carrel shivers. Is he seeing ghosts? Is he losing his mind?

Once again they stand at the base of the last tower: a gaping gully, which he had not noticed before, lies between the four roped-up men and the last rock wall.

"If all four of us climb into the gully, we will meet difficulties getting back," Carrel observes.

"Two of us have to stay here," Gorret recommends.

"In order to affix some rope on the way back."

"I am prepared to stay," Gorret says. Meynet will stay with him.

Carrel and Bich descend into the gully, attain the ridge on the left, and briefly disappear behind the top of the Zmutt Ridge before they reappear on the summit a few minutes later. The makeshift English flag, Croz's shirt, is still flying, and looking at it from afar Gorret is struck by a feeling of unease. The summit team quickly descends via the rock bands on the northwest side and rejoins the others where the arête of the shoulder comes to an end against the final peak.

Giordano observes the summit attack from Giomein. He is convinced that the success is only possible due to Carrel's genius. He writes in his diary: "The summit is covered in cloud. When the fog lifts, we can see our flag on the western summit of the Matterhorn. The English flag now looks like a mere black shawl lying in the snow." Then Giordano makes a sketch of the summit with the two flags and writes "Italia!" next to one.

The following day at noon, the men return to Breuil. They look hale but not like winners. Celebratory flags are flying in Giomein, but Carrel is despondent. It is a very unsatisfying success. He is still convinced that he would have reached the summit before Whymper had he climbed alone that day. Being responsible for the others cost him his victory.

"Great hilarity all day long at the hotel and in Breuil," Giordano notes in his diary. "Bonfires and songs. Amid the rejoicing, I alone was sad; I had not personally climbed the Matterhorn!"

The people of Valtournenche celebrate all night, drinking and dancing, but Carrel and Giordano avoid the party. One because he has lost, the other because he is departing. Important business calls Giordano back to Turin, where he writes to Sella again: "I wish to tell you that, if you wish, you may still climb the Matterhorn and gain some honor to be the first *monsieur* to do it from the Italian side; and if you want, I will go with you."

But Sella does not go to Breuil to climb the Matterhorn. Urgent business prevents him from doing so. On July 20, he moves to the new Italian capital, Florence, where he works on a new draft for a flour tax that is destined to make him famous in Italy due to its great unpopularity.

CHAPTER 24

DEMORALIZED, BACK IN TURIN, GIORDANO is shocked to learn of the tragedy. Whymper's team climbed to the top of the Matterhorn via the Swiss side, but only three of the seven made it back down alive.

One thing is immediately clear to him: the mountain's Swiss name, Matterhorn, will forever be more famous than the Italian name, Monte Cervino. Not because the English reached the top from the Swiss side three days before the Italians, but because the whole world will now talk about the tragedy that unfolded on the descent. This misfortune made Zermatt the most famous village in the Alps overnight. And, cut off from the rest of the world, Valtournenche will remain a forgotten valley forever. Would it be the other way around had Carrel reached the summit before Whymper? Giordano does not think so. It was not a case of an English dandy defeating the mountain man, but rather one of tragedy defeating success. And one of scandal outshining genius.

The tragedy gives Zermatt an unprecedented boost in tourism. In Valtournenche, on the other hand, there is only envy, not increased tourist numbers. Even though tourists appreciate the good food and hospitality of Favre's inn, which opened in Giomein in 1856, visitor numbers are dropping. Valtournenche may be the place from which Whymper and Tyndall launched their first attempts to climb the mountain, and from which the first successful Italian expedition came, but the disaster on the other side gives people more to talk about. "The beauties and terrors of Zermatt's Matterhorn" provide the valley with endless conjecture, endless dramatic stories. It is no longer only the residents of Zermatt, but also its tourists and mountaineers who view the Matterhorn now as the setting of a famous tragedy and claim it as theirs. They all stake a claim in each act of the play: the glorious summit success, the shocking fall, the burning question of guilt. The fact that the Matterhorn is visible, seemingly touchable, from everywhere in the village—from the center, the hotel window, the hiking trail—helps the visitors understand the significance of the tragedy. The recovery of the deceased and their funerals have plunged a whole valley into mourning. Zermatt is crying—even while it experiences an unprecedented boom.

When the Breithorn was first climbed, the first significant mountaineering accomplishment in the Zermatt area, it did not attract any interest. In 1851, the Schlagintweit brothers spent three days on the Col de Saint-Théodule to conduct their geological and meteorological studies, but not a single tourist was interested in them and their doings. But in mid-July 1865, when Whymper is on his way back to England, the Matterhorn is becoming the most famous mountain in the world.

Whymper talks about fate, as if the events in the days before his summit attack were links in a chain of circumstances that would not go with any other story.

The black flag Giordano saw in the snow on the summit was not a sign of mourning but simply a piece of cloth, Croz's shirt.

Back in Breuil, Jean-Antoine Carrel hears about the deaths of two in Whymper's team: young Lord Douglas, who crossed over to Zermatt with Whymper, and Croz, the famous Chamonix guide, with whom Whymper chose to make his daring ascent. There is no news yet about Charles Hudson and Douglas Hadow. Only that four Englishman, who had not all known each other before, had joined forces to master the most difficult first ascent in the Alps. With only three guides!

Carrel feels as if he had personally been involved in the accident. He feels responsible. There is no trace of the schadenfreude that people in Breuil expect him to feel. He feels compassion and is tormented by grief for Croz. For Whymper he feels more respect than anger. Whenever he tries to find an answer to the question of what went wrong, he tells himself that he has no right to judge the Englishman. During later assessment of the accident, Carrel's judgment of the case will repeatedly be out of line with the majority view.

"Whymper is a gambler," Gorret scolds.

"No, he won, and I also had my chance," Carrel responds.

"But your people's safety was more important to you than victory," Gorret says.

"We were also lucky."

"And he was unlucky?"

"Whymper owns the victory, but he also has to live with the worst possible consequences."

Carrel knows that such circumstances could have also befallen his team. This was why he refused to take Giordano. He did not want to bear that responsibility. Safety on the mountain has to be earned, and all his life he has refused to sell responsibility. Being prepared to take risks is acceptable, but being bold just because you are with a mountain guide is not. Just like Whymper, Carrel has a certain sense of selflessness on the mountain, but when it comes to responsibility, their perceptions are completely different.

Slowly but surely, more news about the accident reaches Breuil from the other side of the mountain: "Only three of the seven have survived!"

"Was it coincidence or fate?" Carrel wonders about this, thinking about his commitment toward Giordano and Sella and his refusal to join Whymper.

It seems that after the English climbed the Matterhorn and planted Croz's dark shirt as a flag on the summit, they had descended, all roped together, when Hadow slipped, knocking over Croz, who was in front cutting steps. They both lost their balance, tumbled, and their weight pulled Hudson and Douglas off, sending all four cartwheeling down the mountain. The others—Whymper and the Taugwalders, father and son—survived the fall only because the rope broke, leaving them behind.

Carrel can picture every moment of these tragic events. Every single moment! The images in his mind are clearer than Whymper's memories, and he feels the terror.

"But why did Croz, the strongest, go in front?" Carrel asks himself. It would have been impossible for Whymper and the two Taugwalders to break the fall of four people in the upper section of the northern flank of the Matterhorn!

When they heard Croz scream as he fell, the others gripped the rock as firmly as they could. Whymper watched the four disappear into the abyss and saw how Croz reached out with his hands, trying to save himself. In an instant the four climbers below old Peter were gone, fallen, and swallowed by the mountain.

Again and again, Carrel imagines the events, those fatal moments, and the fall of the climbers seems to him like a fall of heaven. Carrel knows exactly what the survivors must have gone through. He is certain that without an anchor—or the rope breaking as it did—the pull would have been too strong for anyone to survive. He mourns Croz, and he suffers with the Taugwalder family and with Whymper. Victory turned into terror is the worst of all defeats. His own climb now seems to be an unearned blessing.

The body of Lord Douglas was not found, they say. Carrel does not want to think of Douglas as a fallen, lifeless, and disfigured body lying in a crevasse at the base of the mountain in the Matterhorn Glacier.

When and where were the other three buried? They eventually found peace in Zermatt's cemetery, he later finds out.

The tragedy on the Matterhorn has now become the talk of the town in London. Children hear the story at the breakfast table, women talk about it at the hairdresser's, and men discuss it at the club. Europe has been thrown into deep shock—the calamity on the Matterhorn seems to have moved everyone—and for the first time even nonmountaineers take sides. The pros and cons of attempting first ascents is heavily discussed in pubs and clubs, and the debates are emotional, accusing, and perturbing. English newspapers especially are full of accusations. Italian newspapers, on the other hand, report on a rock that pulled the unfortunate party into the abyss, about a gap, a horrible cleft that swallowed them in the end. A German-speaking journalist accuses Whymper of cutting the rope between Douglas and Taugwalder to save his own life.

Such stories, largely or entirely conjectural, spread from editorial office to editorial office, and then from person to person.

The superstitious mountain people are convinced that the expedition was doomed from the start, having never had the blessing of the church. And it had started on the thirteenth of the month and ended on a Friday! Zermatt's village elders believe the accident was a sign from God and that the whole village will soon descend into the underworld of Hades.

On the Italian side of the mountain, the most extreme allegations against Whymper are applauded, and Carrel's reputation is reestablished.

"Isn't Carrel the actual hero?"

"Whymper has to be held accountable!"

In Zermatt, Whymper has no inclination to justify his actions. His oral report about the accident would have to be sufficient. The statements of father and son Taugwalder are identical. For Carrel, it is all clear: whatever the three men report is coherent. It makes sense and is probably truthful.

Still in shock, however, Carrel wonders how Whymper, who had actually contemplated climbing the Matterhorn alone, could have possibly allowed three other Englishmen to join his party, all thrown together by chance, including one lad who did not have any experience on rock. "Unbelievable, this Hadow fellow," he thinks to himself, "tackling the Matterhorn on his first visit to the Alps!"

He views the disaster as more than just tragedy or fate. Could the climbers' passion for the summit and their elation have made them overconfident and careless? Or did things happen as they did in part because it was Whymper's hurried last chance? He must have been able to assess the difficulties of the descent. He was heading a group with a ratio of two guides and a porter to four clients.

Carrel thinks that Whymper lacks a sense of responsibility, but the events cannot be undone.

Apart from Jean-Antoine's circle of friends, his uncle Kanonikus, and Giordano, Sella, and the few members of the CAI, nobody is really interested in Carrel, who with Bich reached his goal exactly on the route where the strongest English alpinists had failed.

"Something needs to change," Giordano says. While Zermatt is still in mourning, the Club Alpino decides to affix ropes on the most difficult sections on the Lion Ridge and build a refuge high up on the mountain for mountaineers to pass the night. Anything to facilitate the ascent. A subscription is started for "hollowing out a cave on the Matterhorn" to serve as a first shelter on the Cravate, where, at an altitude of about 13,524 feet (4,122 meters) overhanging rocks form a natural roof. This is to be done by blasting and constructing dry walls. The once invincible Matterhorn is about to be tamed.

"Carrel's route is far too difficult for tourists," says Giordano. "We have to facilitate and prepare the route for Sunday mountaineers."

In the meantime, Carrel has found out that during the first ascent the English climbed long sections without a rope. Hudson and Whymper were in the lead, partly on the eastern flank and partly on the Hörnli Ridge leading toward Zermatt. They only tied into the rope high up on the mountain and traversed toward the northern side. Whymper wrote, "A rope is not necessary for most of the way."

At the beginning, Zermatt residents expressed euphoria over Whymper's success, but this changed to curiosity and ended in suspicion. In their view, Whymper's victory is a defeat at the same time. It could even be seen as a disgrace for the whole valley. Only the proprietors look at it differently for they know about the power of the press and the public's hunger for horror stories.

"Advantage for Zermatt," Carrel admits.

More and more news reaches Breuil from Zermatt. It is said that, after having quarreled with Carrel, Whymper came to Zermatt on July 12, won over old Peter, and asked him to select a second guide. Back at the Hotel Monte Rosa, Michel Croz was sitting against the wall in front of the building. He told Whymper that he was committed to a man of religion, Charles Hudson by name, and had come to Zermatt to guide him up the Matterhorn. And so had Lord Francis Douglas, who together with Whymper traversed the Col de Saint-Théodule from Breuil. At the Hotel Monte Rosa, Hudson and his friend Hadow had met Douglas and Whymper.

While the people of Valtournenche are still jubilant about the Italian flag flying on the summit of the Matterhorn, news about the disaster is spreading through Zermatt. Not the first ascent but the tragedy is the talk of the town, and suddenly mountaineering comes under fire. Zermatt is filled with grief and anger at the same time, and a feeling of helplessness has descended on Breuil.

When Carrel and Bich reached the south summit on July 17, they saw Whymper's footprints of July 14 but were unaware of the accident. They only learn about it upon their return to Breuil.

Again and again, Jean-Antoine thinks about Whymper feeling helpless, but he cannot see a way to offer support. He can sense how Whymper must feel after having reached the top only to experience disaster. And is he, Carrel, not part of it? Images from the past week on the mountain haunt him even in his dreams, as if Whymper's terror was his own. And Carrel wonders, "How can he live with it?"

CHAPTER 25

"On the Swiss side, climbing La Gran Becca is absolutely terrifying," says Abbé Gorret.

"The northern side of the Matterhorn must be terribly dangerous," the people in Breuil assume.

"The Breuil route must be the better route," a hotel guest observes.

"Whymper left in such a hurry. Is he to blame?" people ask Jean-Antoine Carrel.

"No, he isn't," he responds. "There are many reasons for the accident."

"Tell us one."

"Too many tourists, not enough guides."

"But in the past you've put several people on a single rope."

"My clients are mountain people and they climb as well as they walk. But first and foremost, they allow me to make the decisions."

Carrel says no more.

In Zermatt, the two Taugwalders say that after the accident Whymper was in shock and that he—and they—are only still alive because the rope broke.

"The mountain has taken revenge," the village people say.

When Whymper returned to Zermatt, people report, he met Seiler at the door of his inn. Seiler followed Whymper to his room.

"What is the matter?"

"The Taugwalders and I have returned," Whymper allegedly said, bursting into tears.

It is impossible to talk with him, and as he keeps quiet about the tragedy for a few days, many people view him as a hero.

"He is the only one who made it!" the people say. "The other three Englishmen are dead."

Rumors circulate that the two Taugwalders were petrified and unable to move after the accident.

"This young fellow led them all the way down the Hörnli Ridge to the chalets of Bühl and then carried on to Zermatt."

"How did this courageous man manage to lead his guides to safety?" the people of Zermatt wonder.

"He is the only one of the four Englishmen to come down alive."

Whymper pays the Taugwalders their guides' fee. The elder Taugwalder receives one hundred francs plus a tip of twenty. Son Peter receives eighty francs, and Joseph, who joined them to the bivouac as a porter, gets twenty. For Joseph's return trip from Zermatt via the Col Theodule, Whymper pays him another fifteen francs.

The news that the bodies of the deceased are lying exposed on the Matterhorn Glacier spreads faster than the word about the summit success.

"You can see the bodies from the slopes on the other side," say the people of Zermatt.

Whymper is nowhere to be seen or heard. He has locked himself in his room in the Hotel Monte Rosa and refuses to speak except to beg the local guides to go look for the dead.

Eventually Whymper and the Anglican clergyman Joseph McCormick from Visp quietly make their own recovery plan. They intend to traverse the Hörnli Ridge to the Matterhorn Glacier with a few guides and look for the deceased on Sunday morning. The village priest, Joseph Ruden, obliges all Zermatt guides to go to Sunday Mass, so Whymper puts together a group of Englishmen and guides from elsewhere in the region: McCormick, Robertson (another English clergyman), a Mr. Phillpotts (like Robertson, from Rugby), the guide Franz Andenmatten from Saas-Fee, two guides from Chamonix (Payot and Tairraz, good friends of Croz), and the brothers Joseph-Marie and Alex Lochmatter. The party of nine, including Whymper, departs Zermatt shortly after midnight on Sunday and reaches the perished climbers in the morning via the Matterhorn Glacier, which no one had previously accessed from below the north face. Speechless and pale as sheets, they look at the mangled bodies of Croz, Hadow, and, a bit higher up, Hudson. There is no trace of Douglas.

It's not a pretty sight: smashed skulls, a severed arm, a hand that Payot identifies as Michel Croz's by the scars. The bodies are stripped naked, and tattered pieces of clothing are scattered all over.

Monsieur Seiler in the Hotel Monte Rosa feels relieved when the search party returns, minus the bodies, and Whymper holes up in his hotel room again.

"Whymper is suffering horribly," the hotel rumor has it.

"The poor lad, and he is so young!"

"If the authorities do not allow him to leave soon, he will go insane."

Soon the tragedy is no longer just a rumor, even in the most remote Alpine valleys. John Tyndall reads about it in the papers in Innertkirchen. He decides to go to the Matterhorn and look for the missing Lord Douglas, whose mother, the Marquess of Queensberry, is under the impression that her favorite son is still alive and awaiting rescue somewhere on the mountain. Tyndall hurries to Zermatt, where it is said that he has bought 3,000 feet (900 meters) of rope, intending to lower himself down from the summit of the Matterhorn to recover Douglas's body. Reverend Ruden rejects this plan. "There have been enough fatalities. We do not need any more!"

On July 21, a group of about twenty guides leaves Zermatt with Whymper to recover the bodies.

Up on the glacier, just as they are about to put the bodies into bags, they hear a loud bang from above.

"Rockfall!" one of the guides shouts.

They run for cover. Except for Whymper, who does not move. He continues to look for belongings and equipment in the snow. As if he doesn't mind the grim sight of the dead or fear the falling rocks.

By now, the most unbelievable stories are spreading in the valley. The question of culpability arises, and accusations are made. Not only Zermatt locals attend the funeral; tourists have also come and whisper in the corners. Zermatt mourns and wonders: "Did Whymper really cut the rope to save his own life?"

At the same time, suspicion falls upon the elder Taugwalder. "Was he trying to save his son?"

"Both Taugwalders appeared in court," the priest says in conversation with the innkeeper.

"They went to a hearing," Seiler corrects him.

"Where are the records?"

"Under lock and key."

"Was it not Hadow who caused the accident?"

"He is dead, so he can't testify."

On the other side of the mountain Carrel is asked, "Did Taugwalder fail as a guide, or was the accident Whymper's fault?"

"It is not about guilt, it is about responsibility," Carrel responds.

"Did Whymper really cut the rope when he hurried up to the summit with Croz? If so, the rope would have been too short for the descent and would have had to be replaced by a thinner rope."

"This can't be ruled out," Carrel says.

Carrel's thoughts go around in circles, imagining what it must have been like up there.

He lives the experience as if he is there. He sees that the rope is too short for old Peter to tie in behind Croz, Hadow, Hudson, and Douglas for the descent, so he has to use a spare third rope as he and his son are tied together on the second Manila rope. A little later, Whymper ties in between them. The rope that later becomes the key piece of evidence is thinner and weaker than the other ones.

Which rope was used during the descent is significant. The most important question, though, is why none of the three ropes was fixed. Without such a fixed line, it is probable that even the best rope would have broken after Hadow's fall. It is only because the elder Taugwalder had looped the rope around a rock as an anchor that he did not get pulled off. Only for this reason did the safety rope, which was bound to break, save his life and that of his son and Whymper. Without the strength, caution, and presence of mind of old Peter, none of the seven climbers would have survived.

Carrel is there living the experience again as it happens, as if he is one of the team. When Croz loses his balance and Hadow pulls the following climbers off their feet—the rope having not been taut at this crucial moment—the jerk is so forceful that the guide cannot break the fall.

There were two possibilities: either all seven pulled off the mountain or the rope breaking, as it did. Also, had old Peter also lost his grip, his son and Whymper could not have stopped them all falling along with the others.

Who had determined in which order the climbers would descend? Whymper? Hudson? This decision usually lies with the guides. Being the most experienced guide, Croz should have been at the end of the rope to guarantee the best possible anchor, fixed above the descending party. On the other hand, would they have been able to get off the mountain in reverse order? Croz trusted the Taugwalders and looked after the weakest member of the team, who set the pace on the descent. Everyone knew Hadow's weaknesses.

Carrel imagines himself there on the descent, as yet untroubled. Then Croz suddenly screams and Carrel watches the bodies disappear, witnessing the fall of heaven.

Chapter 26

When he does talk after the accident, Whymper does not say much, and later his published words are nothing but justification. He says the two Taugwalders, the guides, were utterly unnerved and incapable of giving assistance after the accident: "The two men, paralyzed by terror, cried like infants, and trembled in such a manner as to threaten us with the same fate of the others."

"Chamonix! Oh, what will Chamonix say?" he claims old Peter called out. Because no one in Chamonix will actually believe that Croz fell?

"Did Whymper decide that Croz should go first and Hadow second?" Carrel wonders when he finds out more details about the accident.

Did Hudson really climb like a guide? It is only the guides who can be trusted to descend safely on such terrain, Carrel thinks. According to Whymper, Hudson wanted to be third on the rope. Next in line was Douglas and then old Peter—the strongest member being tied on at the end. Carrel sees the mistake in this order.

"The blame, however, lies with nobody," he says.

Least of all with old Peter. The question is whether they were moving all together or whether one person took a step to gain good footing and then had the others follow?

Carrel is convinced that any attempt to hold such a fall—a slip, a jerk on the rope, and four men losing their footing all happening in a split second—would most certainly result in the rope breaking.

Carrel is also certain that old Peter must have been tied onto something. The few moments between Hadow's fall and those of the others that almost rip apart the elder Taugwalder, who has the rope tied around his chest, were not long enough for him to cut the rope or make any other adjustments. It was not even long enough to think clearly.

Of course, everyone would be in a state of shock following such an event, Whymper as much as the Taugwalders. Old Peter at this point would have been less worried about his son and himself than about Whymper, their client, and how to get him off the mountain.

Whymper's story about the descent, claiming that "the Taugwalders had lost all courage," sounds like a tale composed to make him the hero. Which ropes was he supposed to have looped around solid rocks to get the three down? Most of the rope had tumbled into the abyss with the unfortunate four who fell. Whymper claims to have cut some ropes to secure the difficult descent. However, when he describes the Brocken spectre—a magnified shadow of an observer, cast upon the upper surfaces of clouds opposite the sun, a well-known natural phenomenon back then—it becomes clear how confused he must have been: "We were getting ready to descend when, suddenly, an enormous arc formed in the sky, high above the Lyskamm. It was pale and still, but perfectly sharp and clear, except at the extremities, which merged into the clouds and seemed like a vision of another world. Struck with a superstitious fear, we followed with amazement the gradual development of two large crosses at either end of the extraordinary arc."

He claims the Taugwalders had seen the crosses first and thought they had some connection with the fatal accident. Whymper says he was relieved when the eerie apparition disappeared and noted down what was later published in *Scrambles Amongst the Alps*: "The sun was directly at our backs; that is to say, the fog-bow was opposite to the sun. The time was 6:30 p.m. The forms were at once tender and sharp; neutral in tone; were developed gradually and disappeared suddenly. The mists were light and were dissipated in the course of the evening."

But when Carrel talks to young Peter Taugwalder, the guide is unable to remember anything about this supposed "amazing spectacle."

Carrel remembers seeing a similar phenomenon on the other side of the mountain, three days after Whymper had seen it. "We were on the shoulder when suddenly we saw this otherworldly apparition, which was actually a pleasure to watch. In Switzerland, the sky was bright while on the other side in Valtournenche thick clouds were accumulating. We could see our reflections in the center of a circle, which had the colors of a rainbow. We were surrounded by a luminous frame reflecting our shadows."

Carrel also wonders why Whymper came up with additional questions for old Peter after the three survivors had been examined. Did he want to give Taugwalder a further chance to explain?

"No," Carrel decides. "Whymper wanted to blame old Taugwalder for the tragedy."

Whymper seems to have forgotten that he had openly wished to make all decisions on the mountain. According to him, his skills, experience, and courage are equal to those of the best guides and hence, he needs to take responsibility.

"All those who fell were either tied to the Manila or the second rope, which was equally strong," says Whymper, who is supposed to have been about one hundred feet (thirty meters) away from the others when Croz and old Peter tied themselves in to the rope.

Carrel has doubts: "Was it really only Douglas and old Peter who used the weaker rope?"

Which rope linked Whymper to the Taugwalders then? And which ropes did they later leave on the mountain as fixed ropes? To Carrel, Whymper's tangled-up rope story is nothing but lies.

Whymper would write in *Scrambles Amongst the Alps*: "There had only been one link—that between old Peter and Lord F. Douglas—where the weaker rope had been used. This had a very ugly look for Taugwalder for it was not possible to suppose that the others would have sanctioned the employment of a rope so greatly inferior in strength, when there were more than two hundred and fifty feet of the better qualities still out of use. For the sake of the old guide (who bore a good reputation), and upon all other accounts, it was desirable that this matter should be cleared up."

This is an unjustified accusation.

"None of the guides is to be blamed. They followed their duties, however, I strongly believe that had the rope between them been as tight as between myself and Taugwalder, this terrific calamity could have been avoided."

"An excuse," Carrel thinks.

Whymper, who has now come under fire by the international press, justifies his deeds by making the Taugwalders responsible for the accident. He accuses them of cowardice, irresponsibility, and even greed.

Whymper claims that the Taugwalders demanded their pay when they had settled down in their bivouac for the night after the others fell.

"Who will pay us now that we have lost our *monsieur*?"

"Me," Whymper responded.

"Douglas engaged us, and he has always paid well."

"I'll pay you fairly."

"It's okay. Just remember we are poor men and can ill afford not to get paid," young Peter is said to have responded.

"I don't think this is the right time to talk about money," Whymper claims to have said.

"If not now, then when?"

"I shall pay you, of course. Just as if your *monsieur* were here!"

The guides also asked him to write an entry in their guidebook, but Whymper refused. Did he decline because he would have had to be unkind to them? Or because he wanted to make the Taugwalders less credible? In the end, only one version of the Matterhorn tragedy will count—his version.

None of the questions, including Carrel's, will be taken into account: Is it possible that Whymper kept a piece of rope for the descent in order to tie in with old Peter? Lord Douglas must have realized that the leading rope party of four was in a precarious situation. Did he recognize that the men in front would tumble down the cliff if one of them slipped and fell? Why else did he call over to Whymper to move up and tie in with old Peter? However, it is also possible—in fact very likely—that Whymper tied on to the good rope between the two Taugwalders. If this was the case, Whymper must have realized that old Peter was using the weaker rope between himself and Douglas. Why did Whymper only express dismay about the use of the weaker rope later?

Let's travel back in time. On the descent, the entire party is now tied together—Croz, Hadow, Hudson, Douglas, Taugwalder, and Whymper, with young Peter at the back. Such difficult terrain presents a lot of challenges to a team of seven. The team must move slowly since only one person at a time can climb down a difficult section. This slow pace is made worse by fear, as every individual's feeling of insecurity increases with the number of people on the rope. And there is extreme tension because everyone knows that a single misstep can trigger a chain reaction and send the entire party tumbling down the mountain.

Whymper and Croz step on the summit ten minutes before the others. The Englishman stays up there a little longer. He sketches the summit, climbs down to young Peter, and then clambers back to the top to note down on a scrap of paper all the names of the members of this first ascent. He then puts the paper inside an empty bottle, which he leaves between loose rocks. When they rope up for the descent, Whymper ties into the second good Manila rope. Does Croz have any spare rope to fix the difficult sections and leave it there? Is this why old Taugwalder has only the thinner 200-foot rope (60 meters) to tie in with Douglas? Does Whymper still have the long end of the rope slung around his chest as shown in the sketch that shows him in a victory pose?

Nothing is certain. But Whymper, who provided the ropes and considered himself the leader of the party, will not provide any information on that matter. He now refuses to take any responsibility.

On July 17, 1865, the day Carrel reached the summit from the south side, Whymper's friend McCormick wrote to the *Times* in London: "They were descending with great care when Whymper was startled by an exclamation from Croz, and the next moment he saw Hadow and Croz flying downwards. The weight of the two falling men jerked Hudson and Lord Francis Douglas from their feet. The two Taugwalders and Whymper, having a warning of a second or two from the time that Croz called out, planted themselves as firmly as possible, to hold the others up. The pressure upon the rope was too much. It broke and Croz, Hadow, Hudson, and Lord Francis Douglas fell headlong down the slope and shot out of sight over a fearful precipice."

Old Taugwalder's description of the same situation is completely different: "In order to get a better hold, I turn against the mountain, the rope between Whymper and myself is not tight, but fortunately looped around a rock. It holds!"

"This sounds plausible," Jean-Antoine Carrel thinks, and some other mountain guides in Zermatt, are also convinced. Each one of them has at least once held a client, which is much easier on a mild snowy slope than on precipitous rocky terrain like on the Matterhorn, where holding someone's fall is only possible if the holder is tied to an anchor.

Placing himself back in time, back on the mountain, Taugwalder adds: "The fall has put the other rope under such tension that it breaks in the air. I had tied this rope around my body and felt it jerk four times, like several whiplashes. The welts were visible for many weeks."

On July 16, the Swiss newspaper *Der Bund* praises Taugwalder's presence of mind. However, Whymper disagrees: "Immediately after we heard Croz's exclamation, old Peter and I planted ourselves as firmly as the rocks would permit: the rope was taut between us and the jerk came on us both as on one man. We held, but the rope broke midway between Taugwalder and Lord Francis Douglas."

Carrel can only shake his head, when he reads this statement.

Young Peter's description of the situation immediately afterward: "Whymper shivers so badly that he is unable to find sure footing for quite some time." Indeed, Whymper seems to have been in shock during the descent via the east face, continuing to look for his fallen companions, although it was impossible for them to be there; they were lying on the glacier below the north face.

Soon the general public turns from blaming the person in charge of the expedition to accusing two mountain guides. One of those blamed is Carrel, Whymper's mountain mentor. The other is old Peter, the man who saved his life. In Valtournenche, Carrel's position is disputed because he defends

Whymper. Others in the valley want to deny Carrel the monopoly he has gained on the Matterhorn.

On the other side of the mountain in Zermatt, old Peter does not succeed in putting an end to the rumors, not even in his own village. His guiding assignments drop significantly and he is becoming more and more reclusive. "No matter how good of a guide he is, I would no longer entrust him with my life or recommend him to other people," Whymper writes back in London, taking revenge on the man to whom he owes his life. "I'm told that old Peter Taugwalder is now nearly incapable of working. He is not absolutely lost, but his intellect is gone and he is almost crazy."

Croz is dead, Carrel broken, and Taugwalder discredited, only because Whymper can handle words better than he can an ice axe.

Chapter 27

These conflicting reports about the accident cast a dark shadow over mountaineering. The *Times* of London publishes an editorial about the event, which indicates that the interest in the tragedy goes far beyond Zermatt and the alpinists' circles.

> There are occasions on which a journalist must brave certain
> unpopularity and ridicule, even in quarters where it may
> most wish to stand well. We desire the sympathies of the
> young, the courageous, and the enterprising, and we can
> feel their taunts. But we have our Matterhorn to ascend as
> well as they—not without cause. Why is the best blood of
> England to waste itself in scaling hitherto inaccessible peaks,
> in staining the eternal snow and reaching the unfathomable
> abyss never to return? We believe it was the heir presump-
> tive to one of our noblest titles, but, far more than that, one
> of the best young fellows in the world, who fell, with three
> others and a guide, down a precipice of 4,000 feet. A hun-
> dred feet, indeed, would have been enough, but this was

forty times as much. The two English gentlemen who shared his fate, and now another who has perished in the attempt to do in the afternoon without ropes and ladders what he had done with them in the morning, were all just the men England is proud of, and that would be the salt of any age, even more corrupt, more self-indulgent than our own. They were scholars and gentlemen. They were men who had distinguished themselves at school and at college, and in the path of honorable employment. They were admired and loved. The touching notices of the obituary show what fond eyes are now resting on that fatal spot. So many of our readers have "done" Zermatt that it is almost needless to describe the well-known scene. As you stand in that deep valley and look to the southern sky, you see across it, and almost overhead, a vast shelf of rock and snow—a very pathway in the heavens, along which the Olympian deities might be imagined to drive their cars. Upon this shelf stands a mass, in shape between an obelisk and a pyramid, for all the world like an immense ornament of alabaster and frosted silver upon a gigantic marble mantelpiece. A giant might take it up in his hand and place it right or left, as the fancy took him, and they who were heaved to and fro in their beds in that valley nine years ago might think this not so inconceivable. But this charming ornament, this Pelion upon Ossa, is itself loftier than Snowdon. To the humble beholders in the valley below it looks about as accessible as the dome of St Paul's. If compelled to make the choice, we might reasonably prefer to scale with fingers and toes the front of a well-built London house, with good stone window-sills, cornices, and water-courses. If anybody wants to know what 200 feet sheer is, let him go to the top of the Monument. This is 4,000 feet and looks very sheer. As the successful ascent is utterly incomprehensible, of course we do not wonder at the disastrous descent. Indeed, throughout these many hours of continual and painful effort there must have been few places where the climbers could rest their limbs and close their eyes with the momentary feeling of safety. Well, this is magnificent. But is it life? Is it duty? Is it common sense? Is it allowable? Is it not wrong?

There certainly are limits to audacity. We may go even further, and dispute that a wanton exposure to peril is the best school of courage. It is not the best and coolest rider who takes the most headlong leaps. English common sense leaves to young Irish gentlemen the steeplechases in which a certain average loss of man and horse is found necessary to keep up interest. In this island ladies do not like to see a noble horse staked or broken-backed, or a fine young man carried writhing or lifeless from the field. There is a point of danger which, if gratuitous, becomes ridiculous, if not disgusting. Five hundred years ago the young Romans of noble or Papal families thought to revive the glories of the Amphitheatre with bullfighting. "Every champion," says GIBBON, "successively encountered a wild bull; and the victory may be ascribed to the quadrupeds, since no more than eleven were left on the field, with the loss of nine wounded and eighteen killed on the side of their adversaries." No one can read this without a smile at the utter folly of staking the life of a Colonna against that of a wild bull; but a time may come when the historian will tell us irreverently how English noblemen, scholars and divines passed in endless succession to the loftiest peaks of the Alps, accepting the equal alternative of an idle boast and a horrible death. Surely courage, to be respectable, ought to be reasonable, and ought also to have some regard to the end? What is the use of scaling precipitous rocks, and being for half an hour at the top of the terrestrial globe? There is use in the feats of sailors, of steeple-climbers, vane-cleaners, chimney sweepers, lovers, and other adventurous professions. A man may be content to die in such a cause, for it is his life's battle. But in the few short moments a member of the Alpine Club has to survey his life when he finds himself slipping, he has but a sorry account to give of himself. What is he doing there, and what right has he to throw away the gift of life and ten thousand golden opportunities in an emulation which he only shares with skylarks, apes, cats, and squirrels? Life requires a great deal of courage, moral as well as physical, whatever the meaning of distinction. Every gentleman with a sphere of duties and a station in society requires courage and presence of mind, otherwise he is sure to be scorned and become an object of civil contempt. A man cannot hold his own in a parish vestry, or in the committee of a coal fund, without knowing what he is about, and standing to his colours, and defending his rights. If he has not this courage, he had better purchase a lathe, or write metaphysics, for he is good for nothing out of doors. But this courage is not acquired in a succession of desperate adventures. The Age of Chivalry is over. A man does not now learn temperance by a toilsome journey through a desert. By these processes a man only makes himself the slave of a necessity, and reduces himself to the helpless and pitiable condition of being obliged to do something disagreeable, whether he likes it or not. His whole existence centers for the time in that one act or that one suffering, and he can no longer be called a responsible being.

All this, we shall be told, is utilitarian, matter of fact, calculating, coldblooded and so forth. But there is no harm in considering the end and counting the cost. The wisdom of all ages points to the very great advantage of combining discretion with valor, and the immense improvement which valor itself gains by the connexion. Discretion compels a man to contemplate and realize his danger, and to face it, instead of rushing at it with a wild, unthinking impulse and perhaps closed eyes. In these days there is a great waste of energy, that often ends in bringing the impulsive and adventurous into disagreeable collision with their mother earth or a stone wall. When a man of middle age turns to look about him, he sees the path of life behind him strewn with as many sufferers as the half-burnt moths that cover our carpets these summer nights. These are the martyrs of passion. They are the men whose first notion of life was a grand adventure, in which they were to rush at some object or other of which they were enamored, and win it with a blow. That is the theory of human life which is shadowed in these Alpine expeditions. But, of course, our young men will go to Switzerland, and they will ascend mountains, and they will feel a very natural and irresistible desire to do what everybody has done before, and, still more, what nobody has done. This is the great prize which caps and leads on the lesser attempts. It was the blue riband of the Alps that poor Lord Francis Douglas was trying for the other day. If it must be so, at all events in the Alpine Club, that has proclaimed this crusade, must manage the thing rather better, or it will soon be voted a nuisance. They must advise youngsters to practice, and make sure of their strength and their endurance.

"They must take heed to their paths that their footsteps do not slip." They must devise implements of a practical character, unless they are above such weaknesses. They must instill a habit of caution, and calculations as to rests, and such particulars. Above all things, their ropes must not break. If a people chose to despise the aid of improved weapons and defenses as unworthy of a true military genius, it would soon find itself under the heel of its more scientific and mechanical neighbor. We do not see why the Matterhorn must be conquered with sinew alone. With every aid that can be applied it will still be a work of great labor and peril: and we entertain no doubt that the man who submits to be assisted, and incurs no more danger than is necessary, will be a more useful member of society than the other who thought only of the glory of a desperate enterprise. We trust we have not said a word to increase the grief of surviving friends. Our argument shows the value we set on the lives that have been lost. These were no common men, and we could not afford to lose them. They fell into a fashionable rivalry, as was but natural to their time of life and to a forward age. They will not have died in vain if this warning is taken as it is meant.

Abbé Gorret translates parts of this editorial and reads it to Carrel, who shakes his head in dismay and then walks back to his alpine pasture.

CHAPTER 28

ON FRIDAY, JULY 21, 1865, a juridical hearing takes place in the Hotel Mont Cervin in Zermatt. Whymper takes the witness stand first, then Taugwalder. Franz Andenmatten and Alexander Lochmatter, two guides who took part in the first search party, are also being questioned. Whymper's and Taugwalder's testimonies only differ in a few details and in one crucial point: the order of the falling members. Did Hadow pull Croz down immediately as Whymper claims to have observed, or was it Hadow, Hudson, and Douglas dragging the guide down into the abyss, as Taugwalder remembers?

The hearings are presided over by magistrate Joseph Anton Clemenz, the investigating judge of Visp district, and attended by court reporter Donat Andenmatten and ad hoc court servant Johann Julen. The account will go unpublished.

Clemenz asks Whymper to state his name, age, profession, and place of residence.

"Edward Whymper, twenty-five years old, illustrator, residing in London, single."

"On July 13, 1865, did you take part in the expedition that intended to reach the summit of the Matterhorn?"

"Yes."

"How many members took part in the expedition?"

"We were eight when we left Zermatt. We were four tourists, two guides and two porters. On the morning of July 14, one of the porters—one of Peter Taugwalder's sons—left our bivouac and returned to Zermatt."

"What are the names of the four tourists, the two guides, and the remaining porter?"

"Reverend Charles Hudson, Mr. Hadow, Lord Francis Douglas, and myself; the guides were Michel Croz from Chamonix, Peter Taugwalder, father, from Zermatt; the porter was Peter Taugwalder, son."

"What is the home village of Messrs. Douglas, Hudson, and Hadow?"

"Mr. Hudson was the vicar of Skillington, England. The home villages of the other two are unknown to me."

"When did you head out on July 14 for your quest to reach the summit of the Matterhorn?"

"We left our camp at three forty in the morning."

"What time did you reach the summit of the Matterhorn?"

"At one forty in the afternoon."

"How much time did you spend on the summit?"

"One hour."

"Did you follow the same route on the descent as on the ascent?"

"Exactly the same route."

"Were the four tourists and the guides roped together?"

"Yes, in the following order: the guide Michel Croz in front, followed by Hadow, Hudson, Lord Douglas, the guide father Taugwalder, then myself and son Taugwalder at the back. The rope between Lord Douglas and father Taugwalder was thinner than the rope between Michel Croz and Lord Douglas as well as the rope between father Taugwalder and son Taugwalder.

"How did the tragic accident happen?"

"We were descending in the aforementioned order. About one hundred feet below the summit we encountered a difficult section of mixed rock and ice. As far as I know, the only person moving at the time of the accident was Mr. Hadow. He obviously had great difficulty during the descent. For safety reasons, Croz took Hadow's feet, one at a time, and placed them in a safe spot in the snow. I could not say with absolute certainty what actually caused the accident; however, I believe that Michel Croz—after he had placed Hadow's feet onto a rock ledge—turned around to step forward. At that very moment, Hadow slipped and knocked over Croz. The double weight on the rope first pulled off Hudson, then Douglas. While all this happened the three of us, who were a bit higher up, took the opportunity to hang onto the rock with such a firm grip that the rope between Lord Douglas and old Taugwalder indeed broke. For two or three moments we saw our four unfortunate companions slide on their backs and spread out their hands, endeavoring to save themselves, until they disappeared. After the first surprised scream by Michel Croz there was dead silence. The two Taugwalders and myself descended without a further mishap via our ascent route, being extremely careful and constantly looking for the tracks of our unfortunate companions. We could only find two ice axes in the snow! Due to our great care and the search, night suddenly fell upon us at an altitude of about 13,000 feet. We pitched our tent in a spot of a diameter of about 12 feet and continued our descent the following day, Saturday, July 15, 1865. We reached Zermatt at 10:30 in the morning."

"When the bodies were recovered were you on your own or was someone with you? In case you were not alone please state the names of the persons accompanying you."

"Reverend McCormick, a friend of Mr. Hudson's, Reverend Robertson as well as Mr. Phillpotts came with me. The guides Alexander Lochmatter, Franz Andenmatten from Saas Fee, Frédéric Payot from Chamonix and another guide from Chamonix, whose name I don't know, also joined the recovery team."

"Were you able to locate the four bodies?"

"Only three, namely Mr. Hudson, Mr. Hadow, and Michel Croz."

"Did you notify Zermatt's local authorities that you found the three bodies?"

"No, not officially. Upon my return on Saturday morning, though, I notified the mayor of Zermatt about the tragic accident. On this very occasion, I also asked him to send some of his men to the scene in case one of my unfortunate comrades would still be alive. The mayor acted accordingly and an impressive number of guides set out immediately. They returned six hours later and reported that they had sighted the bodies, however, they said that it was impossible to reach them on that very day. On Sunday morning, the same guides refused to go back and recover the remains of the climbers. This was one of the reasons why I did not ask for an official permit when I headed back to find the bodies and did not feel obliged to submit an official report. Everyone who took an interest was informed that three of the bodies were found."

"And there was no trace of Lord Douglas?"

"I found a pair of gloves that I had personally given him in Zermatt, as well as the leather belt that he had worn during the ascent."

"Would you like to make any corrections or add anything to your testimony?"

"I would like to add that from the morning of July 14, Taugwalder's son, who was our porter up until then, served us as our guide."

Edward Whymper reads out the account and accepts and signs it.

Immediately after Whymper's interrogation, Peter Taugwalder, the father, takes the witness stand.

"Peter Taugwalder, forty-five years old, married, guide, residing in Zermatt."

"Did you climb the Matterhorn on July 14?"

"Yes."

"In which capacity did you climb the mountain?"

"As a guide."

"Who engaged you for this expedition?"

"Lord Douglas and Whymper."

"Had you ever climbed with Lord Douglas before the ascent of the Matterhorn?"

"Yes. I guided him on the Zinal and the Gabelhorn."

"Were you informed about who was going to take part before the expedition and did you express your opinion about who should and who should not take part? And were you aware of the disparity between the number of tourists and the number of guides?"

"The number of members was mentioned. I did not have any objections. I did say though that there were not enough guides for the number of tourists. However, when Messrs. Whymper and Hudson responded that they were as good as guides, I did not dare say anything else."

"Who roped up the members before the descent?"

"The four in front—the guide Croz, Hadow, Hudson, and Lord Douglas— were tied in by Croz. I roped up with Lord Douglas on a separate rope."

"Who was the first to tie into the rope?"

"I can't quite remember who Croz roped up first."

"Of what quality was the rope?"

"It was a new, strong rope."

"Who roped you up to Lord Douglas?"

"I did it myself."

"Why was a different rope used between you and Lord Douglas?"

"Because the rope of the other party was not long enough for me to tie in to."

"Do you think the rope between Lord Douglas and you was sufficiently strong?"

"Had I been of the opinion that the rope was not sufficiently strong, I would not have used it to rope up with Lord Douglas. I would not have wanted to put him or myself into danger. Had I considered the rope to be too weak, I would have realized that before the ascent of the Matterhorn and refused it."

"Can you give us a better indication of the place where the accident happened?"

"After we had descended to 650 to 1,000 feet below the summit, we reached the second difficult section of smooth rock where finding a good footing was very difficult. This is where Hadow slipped, first pulling down the men immediately behind him, and then also dragging down Croz after the rope between Lord Douglas and me had broken."

"Are you sure that all safety precautions were taken?"

"Yes. However, it was a real shame that Hadow was such a bad mountaineer."

"How did the accident happen?"

"As I have just told you. I can add that even though Mr. Whymper, myself, and my son had wanted to leave the place of the accident immediately, we remained there for a while. In the end we descended to find a place to pass the night. The following day we arrived in Zermatt, safe and sound."

"Was the rope tight when the fall happened?"

"It was tight."

"How would you judge the breaking of the rope?"

"I don't know. But I think that the weight of three [*sic*] men and the force of the fall would have even broken the strongest rope."

"Do you have anything to add or change?"

"I would like to add that in order to get a better hold I pressed myself firmly against the rock. As the rope between Whymper and myself was not tight, I was able to loop it around a rock, which provided me with the necessary hold to save us."

"Would it have been possible to hold the four men after the rope had broken?"

"Impossible!"

"Could you have saved the tourists if the rope had not broken?"

"I am convinced that together with Croz I could have saved the tourists."

Peter Taugwalder, the elder, reads and accepts the account and signs it.

CHAPTER 29

BEFORE EVEN GETTING BACK TO London, Whymper feels misunderstood and offended when reading the commentary in the *Times*. On July 26, he writes a letter to Edmund von Fellenberg, member of the Bern section of the Swiss Alpine Club, defending his position and portraying his view of the tragedy on the Matterhorn:

> We started at 5:35 on Thursday morning, not intending to go to any great height on that day, but to stop when we found a good position for placing my tent. We took provisions amply sufficient for three days, in case the ascent should prove longer than we anticipated. At 11:50 a.m., we found an eligible situation for the tent, and halted, at a height of about 11,000 feet, sending Croz and the elder of Taugwalder's sons on in advance, in order to save time on the next morning. The remainder built the platform on which we passed the night, and by the time it was finished the two men returned, reported they had seen nothing of great difficulty and triumphantly asserted that had we

gone on with them that day, we could have ascended the mountain and have easily returned to the tent. Well pleased with the intelligence, we retired to our blankets, Lord F. Douglas, myself and the Taugwalders occupying the tent, the others remaining by preference outside; but the sleep which we might otherwise have enjoyed was driven away by the snoring of the Taugwalder family, and long before daybreak we rose, breakfasted, and were ready to start again.

We started on Friday morning at 3:50, leaving the youngest of Taugwalder's sons below, and mounted easily and rapidly. At 6:20 a.m. we had attained a height of 12,800 feet, halted for half an hour and then ascended again without a break until 9:55 a.m., when we stopped for 50 minutes. By this time, we had arrived at the foot of that part which from Zermatt appears perpendicular or overhanging. In reality neither one nor the other, although extremely precipitous.

Thus far we had ascended by the northeast face and had not met a single difficulty, but here we could no longer continue on the same side and therefore went over to the northwest face. For two or three hundred feet the ascent was difficult, and required caution, but as we approached the summit it became easier, and at last it was so gentle that Croz and myself detached ourselves from the others and ran to the top, where we arrived at 1:40 p.m. and the others about 10 minutes after us.

Whymper gives this letter to Reverend Hawker. Feeling a need to apologize, he also writes a letter to Rimini, the secretary of the Club Alpino Italiano. It seems as if he is asking the CAI for absolution, knowing that Jean-Antoine Carrel would have been informed about the tragedy by now. Carrel should also know his view of things: "A single false step, a single slip has been the sole cause of this frightful calamity. The guides cannot be ascribed with guilt nor can they be accused of being careless. Everyone was doing what they were supposed to do. Nevertheless, I am convinced that if the rope had been as tight between those who fell to their deaths as between Taugwalder and myself, the catastrophe could have been avoided."

This note is an attempt by Whymper to absolve the guides of guilt, but he still refuses to take any responsibility.

In the meantime, on both sides of the mountain, the three ropes have become the center of discussion. "As the first five men had been tied while I was sketching, I had not noticed the rope they employed," Whymper will write later in his first written account of the accident. "Now I could only conclude that they had seen fit to use this one in preference to the others. It has been stated that the rope broke in consequence of its fraying over a rock; this is not the case. It broke in mid-air and the end does not show any trace of previous injury."

In initial reports, Whymper's criticism of Taugwalder can be read between the lines, but in *Scrambles Amongst the Alps* six years later he will launch serious allegations: "There remains, however, the suspicious fact that the rope which broke was the thinnest and weakest one that we had. It is suspicious, because it is unlikely that any of the four men in front would have selected an old and weak rope when there was abundance of new and much stronger rope to spare; and on the other hand, because if Taugwalder thought that an accident was likely to happen, it was to his interest to have the weaker rope where it was placed."

At that moment, Whymper had the sole responsibility. He had brought the ropes, he decided how and where they were to be used, and he was the only one who knew their lengths, strengths, and ages. Did he not view himself as a mountain guide? And where was he when the rope party was getting ready for the descent? Making sketches on the summit! Guiding, however, means to take on the entire responsibility, maintain a clear overall view, and keep an eye on every individual. Carrel was the best example of how to take full responsibility, and Whymper had Carrel as a model, having been on the mountain with him. Equally, old Peter was a man of honor who considered the safety of his clients as important as his own. At the very last instant, Whymper tied into the obviously safest place, which was between father and son. Had old Peter not reacted so quickly to the fall, had his strength failed or had the rock holding the loop broken, then he, Whymper, and Taugwalder's son would all have fallen.

Old Taugwalder was responsible for Douglas, and he would never have put his client's life at risk—neither knowingly nor out of negligence. Had Taugwalder borne the sole responsibility, he would have tied his client, not Whymper, to the rope between him and his son. And had Whymper requested it, Croz and Taugwalder would have surely fixed a rope at the place where the accident happened.

On Sunday, July 23, old Taugwalder is summoned for a second hearing. Why only him, and why on a Sunday? Whymper had left but had given the examining magistrate a few more questions to put to Taugwalder.

"Has anything changed in the way you remember things since your last testimony? Do you have anything to add or alter?" Joseph Clemenz asks.

"Nothing! Unless I have not yet told you that I suggested to Croz that before reaching the dangerous place one ought to stretch a rope for greater safety. Croz, however, deemed it unnecessary."

The magistrate does not understand that Taugwalder was talking about a fixed rope, one anchored to a rock above the descending party and used as a sort of handrail for safety. He is generally out of his depth when it comes to mountaineering terminology and techniques.

"Was your son able to see how the accident happened?" Clemenz continues.

"Very unlikely as he asked me, 'My father, are you still there?'"

Clemenz reads out Whymper's next question, "Why were three guests roped up between Croz and yourself, and only one guest between you and your son?" He adds, "The examining magistrate believes that this order does not make sense. How do you respond to that?"

"Guide Croz led the party, followed by Hadow and then Hudson, who regarded himself a guide. Next in line were Lord Douglas, myself, Whymper, and my son. So if you, the examining magistrate, accept that Hudson was acting as a guide, you will see that each tourist was between two guides."

"Did the rope party accept Hudson as a guide?"

"He said that he did not need a guide and could take over the work of a guide."

"Who provided the rope that linked you to Lord Douglas?"

"The tourists."

"Was your son hired as a porter or a guide?"

"On the first day as a porter, on the second day as a guide. Initially, the English *monsieurs* wanted to send my son back, arguing that Croz and I were sufficient as guides. However, due to my request to take my son as a guide, he was eventually engaged."

"What time did you leave Zermatt on July 13?"

"Between five and six o'clock in the morning."

"At what time did you reach your camp?"

"Around noon."

"What time did you leave the camp on July 14?"

"Around two o'clock in the morning. We were delayed by about half an hour. The English *monsieurs* were in high spirits and were laughing."

"In his testimony Mr. Whymper says that Hadow slipped, knocked over Croz, and due to the force the two men dragged Hudson and Douglas with them. In the meantime, Whymper and you two Taugwalders had enough time to secure yourselves. At that very moment the rope broke. In your testimony, however, you state that after Hadow slipped he first knocked over Hudson and Douglas; Croz was the last to slip—after the rope had broken. As Whymper's and your testimonies are not consistent, you are now asked whether you want to maintain your statement."

"As Mr. Whymper was above me and in a better position to give account of the accident, his testimony is likely to be more accurate than mine. This is why I don't necessarily want to uphold my statement that Croz only slipped after the other three had fallen. Everything happened in one single instant. We were so shocked that I am now unable to give an accurate account about the course of events."

"Do you have anything to add or alter?"

"I would like to repeat that I turned away from the mountain in order to find a better hold. As the rope leading to Whymper was looped around a rock and was loose, I had the necessary grip to hold the other rope and save the three of us. Due to the forceful jerk caused by the fall of the others, the other rope cut into my hip so badly that I am still in pain where the rope was tied around my body."

Just as before, old Peter Taugwalder reads, accepts, and signs the written account.

There seems to be someone with a particular interest in the rope failure. It remains a mystery why old Taugwalder was summoned for a second hearing on this matter, on a Sunday of all days, as does the tone of this examination. After all, Sunday rest is paramount in Zermatt.

There is no doubt about it: judging the case is far beyond the capabilities of the court authorities. Is this why the examining magistrate keeps the records of the hearing away from public scrutiny? Is he biding his time for Whymper to write down his own version of what happened?

Back in London the only surviving *monsieur* of the party begins to put the events into words and pictures as he remembers the events, essentially a story of an English triumph, embellishing it with his dramaturgy. England is a world power, and despite all the initial harsh criticism from his home country, Whymper remains English through and through. The two other survivors, the guides, are foreigners and peasants. They speak a patois, a dialect that is difficult to understand. They are able to spell their own names but not much more.

In its statements, which are only made public many years later, the examining commission adapts Whymper's version:

> The committee of enquiry for the district of Visp made up of
> the examining magistrate Josef-Anton Clemenz and recorder
> C. Clemenz, both living in Visp, has reached the following decision
> that there are no grounds for prosecution [regarding] the accident
> that occurred during the descent of the Matterhorn.
> Statements:
> On July 13, at five o'clock in the morning, a climbing party left
> Zermatt in order to scale the Matterhorn. The party consisted of
> Lord Douglas, Hudson, Edward Whymper and Hadow as well as the

guides Michel Croz from Chamonix, Peter Taugwalder father and son, both from Zermatt. On July 13, the team passed the night at the base of the mountain. The following day, they left their camp at 3:40 a.m. and reached the summit at 1:40 p.m. For the descent they used the same route as for the ascent. They were roped up in the following order: the guide Croz was at the front of the rope followed by Hadow, Hudson, Lord Douglas, Father Taugwalder, Whymper and son Taugwalder. At about 300 feet below the summit they encountered a rocky section covered in snow that posed difficulties in finding a good foothold. While crossing this dangerous place, Mr. Hadow slipped and in his fall knocked over the guide Croz. This double weight dragged down Mr. Hudson as well and after him Lord Douglas. The few instants that this lasted gave those at the rear time to secure firm foothold, so firmly indeed that the rope between Lord Douglas and Taugwalder father broke in two. After the tragic accident, the survivors descended very carefully and reached Zermatt without any further mishap on July 15 at 10:30 a.m. after they had passed the night from 14 to 15 July on a small ledge of about twelve feet at an altitude of 13,000 feet.

Given that:

- no criminal offense can be derived from the events described above,
- Mr. Hadow was the cause of the accident,
- [and] on the facts of the case set out above, no one can be accused of a fault or of a crime,

it is decided that there is to be no sequel to the foregoing enquiry, but a decision of no grounds for prosecution, with an order that the State bear the costs.

CHAPTER 30

TURNING A CATASTROPHE INTO A scandal and then into a crime is pretty easy. On July 31, 1865, the author Alfred Meissner from Interlaken, Switzerland, submits an article to the *Neue Freie Presse* newspaper in Vienna. The story is published on August 4, 1865. His account of the first ascent of the Matterhorn makes the reader believe that he was part of the expedition. In reality, though, his entire story is built on rumors. His preamble is nothing more than justification for collecting juicy gossip and making a good story out of it:

> When I returned to my hotel in Interlaken feeling happy and slightly inebriated after the Swiss Wrestling Festival, several travelers had arrived from Zermatt. Their tales brought an air of gloom to my joviality. The horrid catastrophe on the Matterhorn is still the topic of many conversations. But that night, for the first time, I heard a version that made the story even more dramatic.

Meissner hardly knows anything about the tragedy and does not have a clue about safety measures on a mountain. Even though there is no basis on which to pin culpability for the accident and no reason to see it as some sort of moral failure, his article adds fuel to the controversy, inventing details from whole cloth:

> The entire party cartwheeled down the mountain at terrifying speed, but the last three—old Peter, Whymper, and young Peter—were still on their feet trying to halt the fall by wedging their batons in between the rocks. Old Peter had not lost his presence of mind. With his knees clenching a rock, he succeeded in looping the rope twice around his wrist. Whymper and young Peter were also holding back. By now the four in front were dangling in the air, endeavoring to grab onto something that could hold them . . . but in vain. They kept on sliding and soon they disappeared behind a rock in front of the eyes of the remaining three. For about a minute, the men at the back were hovering above the abyss as if they were standing on the roof of a steep tower. Trying to hold the weight of four dangling and wildly gesticulating men, the rope cut old Peter deeply down to his joints and . . . the gravitational force slowly peeled the skin and flesh off his wrist like a glove. But despite his efforts the falling climbers were unable to climb back up again! When his strength slowly left him and the pain of the slicing rope in his arm nearly drove him mad, old Peter allegedly said: "They are dragging us down—we are lost." At that very instant, the rope broke. Or was it cut with a knife that suddenly appeared from behind Taugwalder's back? In short, the men, who had by now become invisible to the climbers at the back, plunged down the precipice. Only two of them could briefly be seen during their fall. They hit protruding rock ledges, bounced back, and continued to plummet. Finally, they came to a halt on a snowfield, 4,000 feet below the scene where the tragedy had commenced.
>
> Three were saved. They continued their harrowing trip, sometimes fixing the remaining pieces of rope to the rocks to lower

themselves. In the evening, they arrived at a safe place on the snow
and even though they were still in shock they were at least able to rest
for the duration of the night. Whymper did not utter a word during
the whole horrendous time.

I am not surprised that the Englishman had lost the ability to
speak considering what he had experienced and witnessed. It may be
true that the self-rescue in that most horrible of moments was justi-
fied, and cutting the rope was an amputation separating those who
were meant to die from those who were still on their feet. Anyhow,
the deed remains ghastly, and living with such a conscience must drive
a person almost insane. The arrival and recovery of the bodies (which
were so badly disfigured nobody dared to actually bring them to the
village) ensued: the following morning at around eleven o'clock, the
three survivors arrived in Zermatt. The search party set out [and]
found the disfigured bodies, and the English priest who had joined
the search retrieved a prayer book from Reverend Hudson's pocket,
prayed Psalm 90 for the deceased, and buried them there and then.
The body of young Douglas was never found.

If it is true what they now say and the break in the rope was no
coincidence, the Englishman will still be able to say: "What do you
want? I had no choice! I acted like a field marshal. I gave up those
who would have plunged us into disaster, and with my quiet deed of
self-help I saved two other lives apart from my own. I was able to give
the father to the son, and the son to the father. What do you want?
Without me all seven would have plunged into disaster." It was a
good thing that Hudson had not brought his steel rope!

Whymper stopped in Interlaken [on his way home]. People who
knew him from before said they found him pretty confused and men-
tally disturbed by the events of the doomed day.

The Swiss media, which stands behind the guides, will deny the
cut rope and hang onto the version that it broke accidentally. However, one thing is clear: the tragedy unfolding on the abyss between
snow and ice goes far beyond the domain of human judgment.

Other newspapers reprint Meissner's report, so it is widely read and discussed. Carrel hears about it but can only agree with the last sentence. Like the Swiss press, he is taking a firm stand against the accusation of the rope being cut. He understands from Whymper's reports and the testimonies of the two Taugwalders that cutting the rope would have been impossible in the circumstances.

Why does Whymper remain silent on that matter? It is very unlikely that he has not heard about Meissner's accusations, but he does not react, and this strategy seems to be successful. Instead of writing rebuttals in letters to the press or trying to prosecute Meissner for defamation, he buckles down and writes his book *Scrambles Amongst the Alps*, which will be published six years after the tragedy on the Matterhorn and then be reprinted into the twenty-first century.

In *Scrambles Amongst the Alps* Whymper first defends old Taugwalder: "Old Peter Taugwalder is a man who is laboring under an unjust accusation. Notwithstanding repeated denials, even his comrades and neighbors at Zermatt persist in asserting or insinuating that he *cut* the rope which led from him to Lord F. Douglas. In regard to this infamous charge, I say that he *could* not do so at the moment of the slip, and that the end of the rope in my possession shows that he did not do so beforehand."

As the footnote continues, however, Whymper casts doubt:

> There remains, however, the suspicious fact that the rope which broke was the thinnest and weakest one that we had. It is suspicious, because it is unlikely that any of the four men in front would have selected an old and weak rope when there was abundance of new, and much stronger, rope to spare; and, on the other hand, because if Taugwalder thought that an accident was likely to happen, it was to his interest to have the weaker rope where it was placed.
>
> I should rejoice to learn that his answers to the questions which were put to him were satisfactory. Not only was his act at the critical moment wonderful as a feat of strength, but it was admirable in its performance at the right time.

Has a broken rope become the symbol for the cold-bloodedness of mountaineers? The question is whether it broke or whether it was cut. If it was cut, who cut it? And why? All kinds of unresolved mysteries for urban newspaper readers, as well as a moral question. Jean-Antoine Carrel, however, will continue to believe that it would have been impossible to cut the rope before it broke, not possible with a knife and not possible with an ice axe. Only those with malicious imaginations accuse Whymper or Taugwalder (or both) of saving themselves by cutting the rope. Both are innocent, but Whymper spends the rest of his life downplaying his responsibility and incriminating Taugwalder. For this, Carrel will never forgive him.

Old Taugwalder, unable to defend himself, does not comment. His pride injured, he does not expect anybody to help him. Whymper's self-defense, which he can only uphold with Taugwalder's silence, steers clear of considering the carelessness with which he dived into his Matterhorn adventures.

CHAPTER 31

IN WHYMPER'S ERA A REMARKABLE number of aristocrats, priests, and wealthy sons of industrialists are enthusiastic about mountaineering. For spiritual men the beauty and power of the mountains must be particularly attractive. Do they feel closer to God atop those peaks? Or is it the silence of the mountains, their mute admonishment, which triggers thoughts about the afterlife? They do not answer the most critical question of the public, though: "Is it reasonable to lead a life motivated by the thrill of deadly risk?" In his justification of his Matterhorn ascent, Whymper evades the moral question of whether such actions are permitted or whether they are actually sinful. Were he to even consider it, his self-image as hero would deny him a thoughtful answer.

Back in England, Whymper is still faced with a lot of trouble. His dream to "conquer" the Matterhorn and become the hero of the Alpine Club has not come true. Being the only surviving Englishman, he has come under fire. He may have been the first person to reach the top, but Lord Douglas, who was a celebrity in England, fell to his death and half the rope party with him. Who is responsible for this calamity? It is not only the press that demands an answer.

The eccentric conqueror of the Matterhorn, who makes old Peter Taugwalder responsible and blames Hadow for the fatal fall, gets no absolution from the public.

Whymper's dilemma becomes clear in his letter to Reverend Richard Glover, who had defended him in a letter to the editor of the *Times*:

Dear Mr. Glover,

Your letter dated 31 July was forwarded to me by a friend, who found it at the Club Rooms; pray excuse my not having replied to it before as I have been overwhelmed by letters. People talk about the vanity of human wishes and we have all felt at some time or another that they are vanity, but never have I felt it as much as I do at the present. For five years I have dreamt of the Matterhorn; I have spent much labor and time upon it—and I have done it. And now the very name of it is hateful to me. I am tempted to curse the hour I first saw it. Congratulations on its achievement are bitterness and ashes, and what I hoped would yield pleasure produces the severest pain. It is a sermon I can never forget.

I saw your letter soon after its appearance and feel obliged for the pains you had taken to place me in favorable light before the public. I could not however help regretting and I am sure you must do so yourself, the reference you made to poor Douglas. A more excellent walker and promising mountaineer I never came across, and had it not been for that final meeting with the others, as far as man can see, we should have made the ascent in perfect safety. What a series of accidents life is altogether! Last year I was at Zermatt intending to go by the same route as we followed this year. I was however obliged by business to return without trying. If it had not been for that I should doubtless have done it then, and we should not most likely have had to deplore this frightful calamity. If again, we had had our dinner on the 12th only half an hour earlier, I should have missed seeing Hudson and Hadow and it might again have been prevented. So far as I am personally concerned I cannot feel myself in blame at all, except for allowing Hadow to go; in other respects, if I had known what was to happen, I think I should have acted exactly as I did.

I am dear Mr Glover,

Yours very faithfully,

Ed. Whymper

In Zermatt, Reverend Robertson had advised Whymper not to make a case of the accident and to avoid polemics. But on August 27—the scandal having turned into a crime, it seems— Whymper complains in a letter to him: "The manner in which I was persecuted by impertinent people on the way home passes all belief. I would have stuck to the resolution I made at Zermatt, had it been possible, but it was not; all kinds of pleasant rumors were propagated and among them it was said that I cut the rope from fear of being pulled over. The amount of silly nonsense that was being written rendered it also desirable that I should write. Therefore, after having read two letters from Wills pressing me to write, two from the editor of *The Times* and a score of others from friends whose opinion I value more or less, I gave way."

CHAPTER 32

THIS IS HOW WHYMPER BEGINS his letter to the editor of the *Times*: "After the direct appeals which I have received from the President of the Alpine Club and from yourself to write an account of the accident on the Matterhorn, I feel it is impossible to remain silent any longer, and I therefore forward to you for publication a plain statement of the accident itself, and of the events that preceded it and followed it."

In the ensuing report, which was published on August 8, 1865, he describes the tragedy on the Matterhorn in detail and from his point of view for the first time.

> On Wednesday morning, the 12th July, Lord Francis Douglas and myself crossed the Col Theodule to seek guides at Zermatt. After quitting the snow on the northern side we rounded the foot of the glacier, crossed the Furgge Glacier, and left my tent, ropes and other matters in the little chapel at the Schwarzsee.

We then descended to Zermatt, engaged Peter Taugwalder, and gave him permission to choose another guide. In the course of the evening the Reverend Charles Hudson came into our hotel with a friend, Mr. Hadow, [and] in answer to some inquiries, announced their intention of starting to attack the Matterhorn on the following morning. Lord Francis Douglas agreed with me it was undesirable that two independent parties should be on the mountain at the same time, with the same object. Mr. Hudson was therefore invited to join us, and he accepted our proposal. Before admitting Mr. Hadow I took the precaution to inquire what he had done in the Alps, and as well as I remember, Mr. Hudson's reply was "Mr. Hadow has done Mont Blanc in less time than most men." He then mentioned several excursions that were unknown to me and added, in answer to a further question, "I consider he is a sufficiently good man to go with us." This was an excellent certificate, given us as it was by a first-class mountaineer, and Mr. Hadow was admitted without any further question. We then went into the matter of guides. Michel Croz was with Messrs. Hadow and Hudson, and the latter thought if Peter Taugwalder went as well that there would not be occasion for anyone else as well. The question was referred to the men themselves, and they made no objection.

We left Zermatt at 5:35 on Thursday morning, taking the two young Taugwalders as porters by the desire of their father. They carried provisions amply sufficient for the whole party for three days in case the ascent should prove more difficult than we anticipated. No rope was taken from Zermatt because there was already more than enough in the chapel at the Schwarzsee. It has been repeatedly asked, "Why was not the wire rope taken which Mr. Hudson brought to Zermatt?" I do not know; it was not mentioned by Mr. Hudson, and at that time I had not even seen it. My rope alone was used during the expedition, and there was first, about 200 feet of Alpine Club rope; second, about 150 feet of a kind I believe to be stronger than the first; third, more than 200 feet of a lighter and weaker rope than the first, of a kind used by myself until the Club rope was produced.

It was our intention on leaving Zermatt to attack the mountain seriously—not, as it has been frequently stated, to explore or examine it—and we were provided with everything that long experience has shown to be necessary for the most difficult mountains. On the first day, however, we did not intend to ascend to any great height, but to stop when we found a good position for placing the tent. We mounted accordingly very leisurely, left the Schwarzsee at 8:20 a.m., and passed along the ridge connecting the Hörnli with the actual peak, at the foot of which we arrived at 11:20 a.m. having frequently halted on the way. We then quitted the ridge, went to the left, and ascended by the north-eastern face of the mountain. Before twelve o'clock we had found a good position for the tent, at a height of 11,000 feet; but Croz and the elder of Taugwalder's sons went on to look at what was above, in order to save time on the following morning. The remainder constructed the platform on which the tent was to be placed, and by the time this was finished the two men returned, reported joyfully that as far as they had gone they had seen nothing but that which was good, and asserted positively that had we gone on with them on that day we could have ascended the mountain and have returned to the tent with facility. We passed the remaining hours of daylight—some basking in the sunshine, some sketching or collecting, and, when the sun went down, giving as it departed, a glorious promise for the morrow, we returned to the tent to arrange for the night. Hudson made tea, myself coffee, and we then retired each one to his blanket bag; the Taugwalders, Lord Francis Douglas, and myself occupying the tent, the others remaining by preference outside. But long after dusk the cliffs above echoed with our laughter and with the song of the guides, for we were happy that night in camp, and did not dream of calamity.

We were astir long before daybreak on the morning of the 14th, and started directly it was possible to move, leaving the youngest of Taugwalder's sons behind. At 6:20 a.m. we had attained a height of 12,800 feet, and halted for half-an-hour, then continued without a break until 9:55 a.m., when we stopped for fifty minutes at a height probably of about 14,000 feet. Thus far we had ascended by the north-eastern face of the mountain, and had not met with a single difficulty. For the greater part of the way there was, indeed, no occasion for the rope; and sometimes Hudson led, sometimes myself. We had now arrived at the foot of that part which from Zermatt seems perpendicular or overhanging, and we could no longer continue on the same side. By common consent, therefore, we ascended for some distance by the arête—that is by the ridge descended towards Zermatt—and then turned over to the right, or to the north-western face. Before doing so we made a change in the order of ascent: Croz went first, I followed, Hudson came third, Hadow and old Taugwalder were last. The change was made because the work became difficult for a time, and required caution.

But where are Lord Douglas and young Peter at the time? Has Whymper forgotten them in his excitement? He may have done as they were obviously there.

In some places there was but little hold, and it was therefore desirable those should be in front who were least likely to slip. The general slope of the mountain at this part was less than forty degrees, and snow had consequently accumulated and filled up the irregularities of the rock face, leaving only occasional fragments projecting here and there. These were at times coated with a thin glaze of ice, from the snow above having melted and frozen again during the night. Still it was a place over which any fair mountaineer might pass in safety. We found, however, that Mr. Hadow was not accustomed to this kind of work, and required continual assistance; but no one suggested that he should stop, and he was taken to the top. It is only fair to say that the difficulty experienced by Mr. Hadow at this part arose, not from fatigue or lack of courage, but simply and entirely from want of experience. Mr. Hudson, who followed me, passed over this part, and, as far as I know, ascended the entire mountain without having the slightest assistance rendered to him on any occasion. Sometimes,

after I had taken a hand from Croz or received a pull, I turned to give
the same to Hudson; but he inevitably declined, saying it was not
necessary. This solitary difficult part was of no great extent, certainly
not more than 300 feet high, and after it was passed the angles
became less and less as we approached the summit; at last the slope
was so moderate that Croz and myself detached ourselves from the
others and ran to the top. We arrived at 1:40 p.m., the others about
10 minutes after us.

I have been requested to describe particularly the state of the
party on the summit. No one showed any sign of fatigue, neither did
I hear anything to lead me to suppose that anyone was at all tired.
I remember Croz laughing at me when I asked him the question.
Indeed, less than ten hours had elapsed since our starting, and during
that time we had halted for nearly two. The only remark I heard
suggestive of danger was made by Croz, but it was quite casual, and
probably meant nothing. He said, after I had remarked that we had
come up very slowly, "Yes, I would rather go down with you and
another guide alone than with those who are going." As to ourselves,
we were arranging what we should do that night on our return to
Zermatt.

We remained on the summit for one hour, and during that time
Hudson and I consulted, as we had done all the day, as to the best
and safest arrangement of the party. We agreed that it would be best
for Croz to go first, as he was the most powerful, and Hadow second; Hudson who was equal to a guide in sureness of foot, wished
to be third; Lord F. Douglas was placed next, and old Taugwalder,
the strongest of the remainder, behind him. I suggested to Hudson
that we should attach a rope to the rocks on our arrival at the difficult bit, and hold it as we descended, as an additional protection. He
approved the idea, but it was definitely settled that it should be done.
The party was being arranged in the above order while I was making
a sketch of the summit, and they were waiting for me to be tied in
my place, when someone remembered that we had not left our names
in a bottle; they requested me to write them, and moved off while

it was being done. A few minutes afterwards I tied myself to young Taugwalder and followed, catching them just as they were commencing the descent of the difficult part described above. The greatest care was being taken. Only one man was moving at a time; when he was firmly planted the next advanced, and so on. The average distance between each was probably 20 feet. They had not, however, attached the additional rope to rocks, and nothing was said about it. The suggestion was made entirely on account of Mr. Hadow and I am not sure it even occurred to me again.

I was, as I have explained, detached from the others, and following them; but after about a quarter of an hour Lord F. Douglas asked me to tie on to old Taugwalder, as he feared, he said, that if there was a slip Taugwalder would not be able to hold him. This was done hardly ten minutes before the accident, and undoubtedly saved Taugwalder's life.

As far as I know, at the moment of the accident no one was actually moving. I cannot speak with certainty, neither can the Taugwalders, because the two leading men were partially hidden from our sight by an intervening mass of rock. Poor Croz had laid aside his axe, and in order to give Mr. Hadow greater security, was absolutely taking hold of his legs and putting his feet, one by one, into their proper positions. From the movements of their shoulders it is my belief that Croz, having done as I have said, was in the act of turning round to go down a step or two himself; at this moment Mr. Hadow slipped, fell on him, and knocked him over. I heard one startled exclamation from Croz, then saw him and Mr. Hadow flying downward; in another moment Hudson was dragged from his steps and Lord F. Douglas immediately after him. All this was the work of a moment; but immediately we heard Croz's exclamation, Taugwalder and myself planted ourselves as firmly as the rocks would permit; the rope was tight between us, and the shock came on us as on one man. We held; but the rope broke midway between Taugwalder and Lord F. Douglas. For two or three seconds we saw our unfortunate companions sliding downwards on their backs, and spreading out their hands endeavouring to save themselves; they then disappeared one by one and fell from precipice to precipice on to the Matterhorn glacier below, a distance of nearly 4,000 feet in height. From the moment the rope broke it was impossible to help them.

The moment the rope broke changed Whymper's life forever. He was still euphoric when he tied in to the rope with the rest of the party. He had just conquered the Matterhorn! Suddenly Croz's scream ripped him out of his dreaminess, and his gaze dropped from heaven down to hell, with his comrades falling into the abyss. It only lasted an instant, and it seemed as if he was tumbling down himself.

For the space of half an hour we remained on the spot without moving a single step. The two men, paralyzed by terror, cried like infants and trembled in such a manner as to threaten us with the fate of the others. Immediately we had descended to a safe place I asked for the rope that had broken, and to my surprise—indeed to my horror— found that it was the weakest of the three ropes. As the first five men had been tied while I was sketching, I had not noticed the rope they employed. Now I could only conclude that they had seen fit to use this in preference to the others. It has been stated that the rope broke in consequence of its fraying over a rock; this is not the case. It broke in mid-air and the end does not show any trace of previous injury.

For more than two hours afterwards I thought every moment that the next would be my last; for the Taugwalders, utterly unnerved, were not only incapable of giving assistance, but were in such a state that a slip might have been expected from one or the other at any moment. I do the younger man, moreover, no injustice when I say that immediately we got to the easy part of the descent he was able to laugh, smoke, and eat, as if nothing had happened. There is no occasion to say more of the descent. I looked frequently, but in vain, for traces of my unfortunate companions, and we were in consequence surprised by the night when still at a height of 13,000 feet. We arrived at Zermatt at 10:30 on Saturday morning.

Immediately on my arrival I sent to the President of the Commune, and requested him to send as many men as possible to ascend heights whence the spot could be . . . where I knew the four must have fallen. A number went and returned after six hours, reporting they had seen them, but that they could not reach them that day. They proposed starting on Sunday evening so as to reach the bodies at daybreak on Monday; but, unwilling to lose the slightest chance, the Rev. J. M'Cormick and myself resolved to start on Sunday morning. The guides of Zermatt, being threatened with excommunication if they did not attend the early mass, were unable to accompany us. To several, at least, I am sure this was a severe trial: for they assured me with tears that nothing but that which I have stated would have prevented them from going. The Rev. J. Robertson and Mr. J. Phillpotts of Rugby, however, not only lent us their guide, Franz Andenmatten, but also accompanied us themselves. Mr. Puller lent us the brothers Lochmatter; F. Payot and J. Tairraz, of Chamonix, also volunteered. We started with these at 2 a.m. on Sunday, and followed the route we had taken on Thursday morning until we had passed the Hörnli, when we went down to the right of the ridge and mounted through the seracs of the Matterhorn Glacier. By 8:30 a.m. we had got on to the plateau at the top, and within the sight of the corner in which we knew my companions must be. As we saw one weather-beaten man after another raise the telescope, turn deadly pale, and pass it on without a word to the next, we knew that all hope was gone. We approached; they had fallen below as they had fallen above—Croz a little in advance, Hadow near him, and Hudson some distance behind; but of Lord F. Douglas we could see nothing. To my astonishment, I saw that all of the three had been tied with the Club, or with the second and equally strong rope, and consequently there was only one link—that between Taugwalder and Lord F. Douglas—in which the weaker rope had been used.

The letters of Rev. J. M'Cormick have already informed you respecting the subsequent proceedings. The orders from the Government of the Valais to bring the bodies down were so positive, that four days after the events I have just related twenty-one guides accomplished that sad task. The thanks of all Englishmen are due to these brave men, for it was work of no little difficulty and of great danger. Of the body of Lord F. Douglas they, too, saw nothing; it is probably arrested in the rocks above. No one can mourn his loss more deeply or more sincerely than myself. Although young, he was a most accomplished mountaineer, hardly ever required the slightest assistance, and did not make a single slip throughout the day. He had only a few days before we met made the ascent of the Gabelhorn—a summit considerably more difficult, I believe, to reach than the Matterhorn itself.

I was detained in Zermatt until July 22, to await the inquiry instituted by the Government. I was examined first, and at the close I handed into the Court a number of questions which I desired should be put to the elder Taugwalder; doing so because that which I had found out respecting the ropes was by no means satisfactory to me. The questions, I was told, were put and answered before I left Zermatt; but I was not allowed to be present at the inquiry and the answers although promised, have not yet reached me.

This, Sir, is the end of this sad story. A single slip, or a single false step, has been the sole cause of this frightful calamity, and has brought about misery never to be forgotten. I have only one observation to offer upon it. If the rope had not broken you would not have received this letter, for we could not possibly have held the four men, falling as they did, all at the same time, and with a severe jerk. But, at the same time, it is my belief no accident would have happened had the rope between those who fell been tight, or nearly as tight, as it was between Taugwalder and myself. The rope, when used properly, is a great safeguard; but whether on rocks, or whether on snow or glacier, if two men approach each other so that the rope falls in a loop, the whole party is involved in danger, for should one slip or fall he may acquire, before he is stopped, a momentum that may drag down one man after another and bring destruction to all; but if the rope is tight this is all but impossible.

I am, Sir, your obedient servant
Edward Whymper
Haslemere, August 7

This account reads like a sincere apology. It is Whymper's successful attempt to change the course of events in his favor, reject all responsibility, and put all blame on the Taugwalders. Some parts are debatable. Had old Taugwalder not remained calm and fixed the descent route after the accident, which had badly shaken young Whymper, the Englishman would have been out of his depth trying to descend. Already during the ascent, the two guides had noticed that there were few opportunities to fix a rope for the descent. Surely, Croz should not have gone in front of the descending party, but had he done otherwise, how would he have been able to get his clients down the mountain—particularly the climbing novice Hadow?

CHAPTER 33

WHEN MORE THAN FIFTY YEARS later, the younger Peter Taugwalder, the son, now seventy-five years old, finally gives his account of the climb, it is too late to undo the damage done to his father. The younger Taugwalder submitted his version of what happened to Theophil Lehner, who wrote it down in a comprehensive and realistic way.

> I remember many things so vividly, as if it had happened only yesterday. The impression this terrible tragedy left is so strong that I will never forget it for as long as I live.
>
> It was in the first half of July of said year when young Lord Douglas came to Zermatt to undertake several climbing expeditions guided by my late father; the first ascent of the Obergabelhorn, amongst others. He had the intention to be the first to climb the Matterhorn, as well. It was then, on July 10 or 11, when Chamonix guide Michel Croz arrived at the Hotel Monte Rosa, accompanied by the Englishmen Whymper, Hadow and Hudson, who had the very

same intention to complete the first ascent of the Matterhorn. After hearing their plans, Lord Douglas and his mountain guide [old Peter] decided to join the group.

At that time, I was indeed very young; I had merely started growing the first facial hair on my upper lip. However, I was courageous enough to feel that no rock wall was too high, no glacier too steep. At only 16, I had already climbed the Monte Rosa, together with three British students and my father. He did not want me to go with them, because he feared that it would be too cold for me. I must tell you, the Monte Rosa was a notoriously cold mountain; many have lost their toes climbing it. Nevertheless, I insisted to go with them, since I was the one who convinced the students to attempt the ascent. This is why they were just as much my clients as they were my father's. And I told him that if he did not want to lead the said ascent, I would find another guide who would. Long story short: I went with them and it was a great success; my joy alone would have carried me to the summit.

But to come back to the main subject. When it came to mountaineering, I was not an amateur anymore. At the time, I had already under my belt the ascent of the Breithorn and several others, which is why I suggested to my father that he let me accompany them. Originally, he had planned on hiring two additional mountain guides, creating two roped parties, but his idea did not please Mr. Hudson; he, the humble man he was, believed that he and his companions were more skilled than the mountain guides.

In the morning of July 13, we fetched the necessary provisions from the Hotel Monte Rosa and started our journey at around nine o'clock. The weather was wonderful; the Matterhorn, completely free of snow, was warmly welcoming us in the morning sun. We had lunch on the Hörnli. The views were magnificent; we were surrounded by great, majestic summits. Above the green of the valley, the dark scots pines thronged to the edge of the eternal ice. My heart was pounding out of joy and I could barely await the next morning. When we reached the foot of the Matterhorn, we pitched our tents and camped. Croz and I climbed quite a bit higher to approximately the same spot where they later built the so-called Altes Refugium ('Old Refuge'). Everything went without a glitch and we did not have the slightest difficulties. We returned to our companions and told them the good news. We enjoyed the soup the others had prepared in the meantime and eventually laid our heads on our knapsacks to get some rest. I slept like an angel.

All night I dreamt about standing on top of the Matterhorn, sending a yodel down into the valley loud enough to be heard in all of Zermatt. And then, suddenly, I was alone on the summit. I was not able see the others, and the terror of that woke me up. It was about two o'clock and the others had started to wake up, as well. We made some tea after which we started our attack of the enormous peak before us. Of course, we roped up immediately; Croz led the party, followed by Hudson, Whymper, and Hadow, then my father, Lord Douglas and me. At about three o'clock, the day began to dawn and the sky in the east was shimmering like pure gold. There was not a single cloud in the sky; the only audible sounds were the steps of seven passionate mountaineers and the clattering of the ice picks on the rock.

We followed the same route Croz and I had reconnoitered the night before. Everything went smoothly until we reached the bit above the place where the Old Refuge is located today. From that point onward, the level of difficulty started increasing, but we were all of good cheer and able to quickly gain height. About 150 feet above where today's Solvay Refuge is located, we rested and had a little something to eat to restore our strength. Then, we attacked the shoulder, into which Croz carved steps. Douglas, who was in front of me, had great difficulty placing his feet on the steps and several times he slipped. But for most of the time I pressed his feet firmly into the steps. Finally, we reached the shoulder. We left our knapsacks and provisions at the very top; nowadays that is where the fixed ropes begin. We deliberated on the route we should take to overcome the most challenging part of the climb. We knew that it would get easier once we were above the roof. Croz was the one who took the decision to cross over to the west face, the so-called 'in d'Lätzi' ('shady slope'). It was entirely free of snow, and there were small naturally formed steps about one or two inches wide; we used them to climb our way up. Below us was a 6,000-foot vertical drop, as steep as it gets. Not a word was uttered while we were cautiously and tensely climbing up. We were all very well aware of the seriousness of the situation.

Just one wrong movement or one wrong step, and our bodies could have ended up down on the glacier, dashed to pieces. I was young and agile and I climbed the mountain like a cat climbs a tree. I was always able to observe the others and to secure Lord Douglas's feet for him. He was not the best mountaineer. Slowly but surely, we safely made our way up; finally, we reached the bit above the roof and at around two o'clock we reached the summit.

We did not stay for long. My heart was so light, and I felt like I could have flown far away, above and beyond the mountains, maybe even down to Zermatt to see my sweetheart. Then, we made ready for the descent. Whymper traded places with Lord Douglas and was now directly in front of me on the rope. Croz was still leading the group. So we slowly climbed down across the roof at approximately the same section where the descent still crosses today. After that, we traversed back to the west face along a ledge. We moved very slowly and with the utmost caution, since the descent was considerably more difficult than the ascent. We got to the end of the ledge, where Croz started to climb down the north face together with the three men closest to him. From time to time, my father belayed the rope on a ledge.

All of a sudden, the four climbers shot through the air, almost as if they were leaving behind a small cloud where they used to stand. The rope broke as if it had been a mere thread; the four young mountaineers were gone. It happened as fast as lightning strikes. No one made a sound. They had disappeared into the dreadful abyss.

One can only imagine how we felt. We were barely able to move—that is how shocked we were. Eventually, we tried to continue our descent; but Whymper was shaking so much, he was almost incapable of taking a step forward. My father took the lead and kept turning around in order to secure Whymper's feet while climbing down the steps. We had to stop repeatedly to rest, for we were deeply shaken by what had happened. Nevertheless, we kept going and eventually, we were back on the ridge, where we tried to eat something; it was virtually impossible, though. Our throats felt as if we were being [choked], incapable of swallowing anything. This was not surprising, since farther down we saw our unfortunate companions lying on the cold ice of the glacier. . . .

And only if the kind Mr. Douglas had not traded places, then he would have been the one who survived; he would well have been a better and more loyal friend to us than this Mr. Whymper, who had been so very unapproachable and distant—and still was afterwards, even though we had saved his life. Without us, he would have died, as well. Without a doubt! He later told a different story, a story in which he was the hero, and he said things that were not true. I, for instance, never saw any of the three crosses Mr. Whymper had allegedly spotted in the sky. Furthermore, he put words into our mouths, without any motivation. How could he have understood any of the things we were saying? He did not speak a word of German, and my father spoke no other language besides a dialect native to Zermatt.

But let's go back to the descent. We fetched the knapsacks and then, with great difficulty, made our way to a snow-free spot below the ridge, where we spent the night, sitting down. Just before dawn, the temperatures were very low, despite having been quite moderate in general. As soon as we had enough daylight, we continued the descent. We did not encounter any further difficulties; once we were on the move, we regained our agility, although we only reached Zermatt around three o'clock.

Upon arrival we went to Father Seiler at the Monte Rosa to tell him about the tragic incident. Measures were immediately taken to recover the remains of the deceased. It was a Saturday, and because they were all undoubtedly dead, there was no need for anyone to set out for the mission at night. The rescue team waited for the day to dawn before leaving Zermatt. I was not able to accompany them; I was still very much in shock. Whymper and my father were not able to go, either.

The search party found our poor friends on the glacier, at the very spot we had indicated. Only Lord Douglas was missing—and until this day his body's whereabouts remains unknown. They had all been dashed to pieces, Croz being the worst case of them all. They had lost most of their clothes. A few days later, the whole community attended their funeral at the cemetery of the tiny Zermatt church.

I have climbed the Matterhorn over one hundred times ever since, but never without thinking about my dear comrades who lost their lives in a terrible accident that day. My father and Whymper have already joined them in heaven, and soon, the angels of death will call for me, as well.

CHAPTER 34

JEAN-ANTOINE CARREL'S ROUTE TO THE summit of the Matterhorn poses significantly more difficulty than Whymper's. But the locals of Valtournenche still expect tourists who prefer to climb the mountain from their side, which may be more challenging but is certainly safer. The canon of Aosta, who views tourism as a good way for the poor mountain people to earn extra income, suggests constructing a hut halfway up the Lion Ridge. The CAI adopts this idea and asks its members to come up with the necessary funds. Carrel, who proposes to build it at the natural cave on the Cravate at 13,524 feet (4,100 meters), is in charge of the construction. In autumn 1865, the tiny shelter is finished and ready to use.

After the Matterhorn tragedy of 1865, the authorities did not, as expected, impose a ban on climbing the mountain, but it is not until August 1867 that the Lion Ridge is attempted for the second time. The rope party consists of Florence Crauford Grove along with three people from Valtournenche, namely Carrel, Bich, and Meynet. They pass the night in the drafty CAI hut, climb the exposed ridge up to just below the Great Tower, and traverse via the northwest side to the Zmutt Ridge, following Carrel's first ascent route. This route to the top is difficult and also dangerous in places. No man other than the ingenious Carrel could have established it, and no other people than the locals, with their knowledge of the terrain and their chamois-like instincts, are courageous enough to take tourists up this route.

The natives of Valtournenche are delighted that Grove's ascent is made from their side of the mountain. Some of them, however, are not pleased about Jean-Antoine Carrel's monopoly on the mountain. Is this why one month after Grove's successful ascent three of the Maquignaz brothers plus César Carrel, Jean-Baptiste Carrel, and Jean-Baptiste's daughter set out to find their own route to the summit? After all, the other guides want their share in the profit from tourism. On September 12, they climb to the Höhlen Hut, where they pass the night. While one of them stays behind the following day, the five others climb the shoulder to the cleft where Bennen and Tyndall were forced to retreat in 1862, and they traverse it. They are now standing right in front of the last precipice: a gigantic bulwark! Instead of deviating to the left to the Zmutt Ridge like Carrel and Grove did, Joseph and Peter Maquignaz tackle the summit rock directly. To this very day it remains a mystery how they accomplished this. It is very likely that this Alpine masterpiece was achieved from above by applying incredible skill as well as ladders and wooden poles. This route is shorter and less dangerous than Carrel's, and, facilitated by fixed ropes and ladders, it later becomes known as the normal route from Breuil.

On the east side of the mountain things have not been idle either. Another hut is constructed, at an altitude of 12,526 feet (3,818 meters) on the ridge descending toward Zermatt. This is done at the expense of innkeeper Seiler and the Swiss Alpine Club. The execution of the work has been placed under the direction of the Knubels of the village of St. Niklaus. The next addition is the Hörnli Hut, which is built at the base of the mountain. On July 24 and 25, 1868, Peter Knubel and Joseph Maria Lochmatter, from the same village, lead Julius Marshall Elliot up the Matterhorn from the Swiss side, making the second ascent of the Whymper route.

Carrel and the Lion Ridge have a special attraction for tourists, some sort of additional magnetism. Florence Crauford Grove, for example, speaks very highly of Jean-Antoine: "I respect him for his admirable courage as well as for the care and attention he gives to his clients. He does everything to avoid even the possibility of an accident."

People in the village, on the contrary, are getting increasingly envious. Three days after Lochmatter and Knubel reach the top, John Tyndall climbs the Matterhorn on his third attempt, with two of the Maquignaz brothers as guides, and they make the first traverse from Breuil to Zermatt. "The two Maquignaz brothers are excellent companions, calm in dangerous situations and strong, where you need strength," the professor writes in the brothers' book of recommendations. A week later, François Thioly and O. Hoiler traverse the Matterhorn from the opposite direction, from Zermatt to Breuil, also with guides from Valtournenche. And, in the same season, on September 4, Felice Giordano finally reaches his longed for summit, having engaged the best guides in the valley, namely Jean-Antoine Carrel and Jean-Jacques Maquignaz. At the end of July 1866, together with Carrel, Bich, and Meynet, he had gotten as far as the Cravate, where he hunkered down for one week to take measurements. At that time, Carrel had decided against a summit attack. Now, two years later, Giordano connects the paths of Carrel and Whymper and unites the rival guides from the two valleys to form a partnership of convenience.

Over the following years, progress is made on the mountain. The ascent routes on both sides of the Matterhorn are fixed. Lucy Walker becomes the first woman to climb the Matterhorn in 1871. And ascents are undertaken without guides beginning in 1876.

In 1877, twelve years after the first ascent, Quintino Sella, now fifty years of age, and his sons attempt to climb the mountain. Perhaps needless to say, they engage Jean-Antoine Carrel. During the climb, the fixed rope nearly leads to disaster, and it is only thanks to Carrel's instinctive reaction that a tragedy similar to the one in 1865 is avoided. When everyone is tied into the rope behind Carrel, he advances to examine the state of the fixed rope just below the ladder. He free climbs the rock next to the rope to check the conditions, and suddenly slips. When Carrel grabs the fixed rope, it breaks, causing him to turn and fall past Sella's head without touching him. For a moment he seems to float. He plunges approximately 150 feet (45 meters) and then succeeds in breaking his fall by springing onto a rock like a cat. He hugs the rock, finds firm footing, and comes to a halt on a ledge, petrified.

Terrified, Sella holds the rope everyone is tied into.

The second client member of the Sella team, Antonio Castagneri, who has joined this expedition with his guide Jensing, is now forced to watch Jensing struggle to climb this short section without a rope—successfully. However, as soon as Carrel has recovered from his fall, he takes Jensing on the rope and leads him up along his own bloodstains. Carrel's ability to concentrate, his feline climbing skills, and his sense of responsibility have become a legend. Sella sings his praises just as he sings praises about the mountain:

> Jean-Antoine is like the Matterhorn. You cannot even begin to comprehend this kind of beauty. I used to think that I knew the mountains, their appeal and their poetry. But when I climbed the Matterhorn, I had to acknowledge that I did not know a thing— that's how different this unique piece of rock is. It is superior to all other mountains. You may scold me, but shall the opportunity arise again, I will go back and climb the Matterhorn a second time. What does this little bit of danger mean? Up there you can't really hurt yourself or become a cripple. One single slip of the foot means certain death, sending you tumbling down for more than a mile. Could one ask for a better way to finish life?
>
> I only regret having taken my sons. I have already lived half a century and the loss of my life would not be a great demise for Italy. It would be a shame, however, if our country would lose such young and strong people. Carrel and his guiding skills alone boosted their morale. They were so happy and enthusiastic about the fascinating spectacle! You can still see the sparkle in their eyes when they talk about it, even today!

Following two failed attempts, the famous photographer Vittorio Sella, nephew of Quintino Sella, will reach the summit in March 1882—completing the first winter ascent.

Despite the controversy of 1865, the English are proud of their climbers' successes—and finally proud of Whymper. Climbing the Hörnli Ridge has become a must for all serious alpinists. The Matterhorn has turned into a myth and Whymper into a legend. Albert Mummery revolutionizes alpinism by climbing without guides, the Pendelbury brothers scale the east face of the Monte Rosa in 1872, and sport alpinism as introduced by Whymper becomes socially accepted. The east face of the Monte Rosa—a gigantic wall of mixed rock and ice towering almost 10,000 feet (3,000 meters) above the valley of Macugnaga— is now considered the most challenging and dangerous climb. Due to its technical difficulty and extraordinary dangers of serac and rockfall, this route is feared and sought at the same time.

The winner of the race to the top of the Matterhorn gives in to the demands of the established members of the Alpine Club and takes up scientific work. He is still the well-respected engraver, but his interests have shifted from making first ascents to researching glaciers. In order to do some scientific research on snow, Whymper launches his first expedition to Greenland in 1867.

In 1872, the magazine *Echo des Alpes* reports about some Matterhorn relics on display in Zermatt:

> When we said goodbye to Mr. Seiler just before our departure from Zermatt, we asked him to show us the remaining effects of the men who died in 1865. At first we saw the rope that was used between Father Taugwalder and Lord Douglas. Bloodstained, it was made of a weird plait and looked like a washing line as thick as a little finger. The point where it broke looked like a paintbrush, indicating that it was certainly not cut with an ice axe. A second object—a worn-out boot with a torn sole that still stuck to the heel—was identified as belonging to Douglas, whose body was never found. A woolly rag approximately as wide as two thumbs, which is attached to the inside of the shoe, was supposed to have alleviated the pain from an injury the lord had been suffering from for weeks.

And Mummery sets to tackling the Matterhorn in novel ways. On September 3, 1879, he makes the first ascent of the mountain via the Zmutt Ridge, and on July 16, 1880, he attempts to be the first to climb the mountain via the Furggen Ridge. In the latter effort he doesn't succeed. After he advances to the height of the Swiss shoulder, he then traverses the east face, reaches the Swiss ridge at a point where the shoulder is attached to the head of the mountain, and continues the normal route all the way to the top.

CHAPTER 35

YEAR BY YEAR, THE NUMBER of successful Matterhorn climbs continues to rise, with more ascents being undertaken from Zermatt than from Breuil. In 1871, Whymper publishes his book about his mountaineering adventures. Well written and brilliantly illustrated with his own woodblock prints, it is now a classic that provides the most widely known images of the first ascent of the Matterhorn. The book, Whymper's justification and settlement questions, can be read as a firsthand adventure. However, in 1871 it also provokes existing animosities and kindles new accusations. Whymper does not like the Taugwalders, and the Taugwalders do not like Whymper, which is an open secret in Zermatt. But who actually does like Whymper? Certainly nobody in Zermatt. Whymper manages to stir up the close-knit spirit and competitiveness in the valley with his interpretation of the accident. Old Peter suffers psychologically, falls into depression, and withdraws more and more, while Whymper basks in his success. Every year he returns to the Alps, the playground of his triumphs. Again and again he visits Zermatt, Chamonix, and Valtournenche.

Before the accident in 1865, old Peter Taugwalder's reputation was untarnished, and after the accident this continued for a time. Not two months after the first ascent, the shock still in his limbs, he guided twenty-five-year-old Peter Güssfeldt, who later became the advisor of Kaiser Wilhelm II and one of Germany's most accomplished mountaineers, via the Whymper route. "Taugwalder had been on the summit," Güssfeldt later writes. "He must know the way, and I will pay him a high salary. However, when I approach him with my plan he looks horrified, tries to talk me out of it, and shows me the scars where the rope cut into his flesh."

Nevertheless, Güssfeldt succeeds in persuading the two Taugwalders. They agree to climb from Breuil, not from Zermatt, but the route proves too hard for Güssfeldt. He capitulates just below a vertical rock face and disappointedly orders everyone to turn back. "After a 21-hour hike with only a few breaks we arrived in Breuil at eleven o'clock at night. A hard-fought-for failure."

John Ball, natural scientist and first president of the Alpine Club, affirms old Peter but tempers the praise, saying, "Peter Taugwalder is a better guide than many others I have met. He is a first-class rock expert, strong, willing, but sometimes a bit stubborn." In his day, Taugwalder is one of the most experienced guides in the Alps and the most successful one in Zermatt. Renowned English alpinist Francis Fox Tuckett, president of the Alpine Club from 1866 to 1888, hired him, and in 1862 he guided Kennedy during his attempt to climb the east face of the Matterhorn in winter. Just a few days before the 1865 tragedy he made the first ascent of the Obergabelhorn from Zinal. Lord Francis Douglas, whom he guided up the Obergabelhorn, wrote in his journal: "Peter Taugwalder is very skilled and has proved to be a first-class guide." Apart from Peter Perren, he was the only other Zermatt guide who was convinced, before the fact, that the Matterhorn was scalable.

But in the end, the senior Taugwalder's career as a Matterhorn guide falls victim to Whymper's insinuations. His insisting on old Peter's "insanity" seems to have a negative effect on the guide's business. In 1867 a Matterhorn aspirant arrives in Breuil and writes: "Father and son Taugwalder are here and prepared to climb the mountain from Zermatt with me." Then it is as if the writer's eyes fall upon the Maquignaz brothers, who are just coming down the mountain. "However, as I would like to do a traverse of the Matterhorn, I prefer to engage guides from Italy." The Taugwalders are dismissed.

It is inevitable that immediately after the tragedy, the Zermatt guides steer clear of their mountain for a while. In 1869, the two Taugwalders and Perren take R.B. Heathcote on an attempt to climb the Matterhorn from Breuil. They have a close call with lightning before they reach the summit, but fortunately they all survive.

It takes young Peter seven years before he returns to the site where the fatal tragedy unfolded. He is guiding the Pendelbury brothers and Charles Taylor, who have just scaled the biggest wall in the Alps, namely the east face of Monte Rosa, with their Saas guide Ferdinand Imseng. On July 24 and 25, 1872, old Peter—Matterhorn Peter, as he is now respectfully called—traverses the Matterhorn summit from Zermatt to Breuil with them.

While it becomes increasingly difficult for old Peter to find clients as he ages, his colleagues, equipped with ice axes and ropes, are busy leading guests up the mountain from the Zermatt side. He no longer gets guiding assignments and is fed up with sitting on the little wall where the guests engage their guides. He does not want to feel redundant or be exposed to stares and awkward glances, and he soon stops going out. Instead he stays home, smokes his pipe, drinks his wine, and falls deeper and deeper into depression. Nobody knows what is going on in his mind, but one can guess. In 1867, his second son, Joseph, drowned in the Schwarzsee. It was Joseph who carried Whymper's equipment, including the ropes that were eventually used for the first ascent, from Breuil to the little chapel at the Schwarzsee in 1865.

One day Old Peter's wife packs a few clean shirts, socks, and some food for him. In semi-darkness he just stands there, as calm as always, gazing out the only window in the kitchen, staring into the distance. Nobody talks, nobody cries. His wife sighs as if resigned that it is for the best, even for her. Then without a single word, just a handshake, he takes his rucksack and leaves the house—bound for America. Peter Taugwalder's third son, Friedrich, who was fifteen years old when he accompanied the 1865 expedition to the first bivouac, accompanies his father to America.

The elder Peter returns to Zermatt a few years later, minus Friedrich, who stays in America. The old man seems even more reclusive now, and nobody knows what he did while he was away. It seems as if the Taugwalders have no other choice but to flee a curse from Whymper, the man whose life old Peter once saved.

When a consortium of Zermatt citizens builds the Hotel Schwarzsee, old Peter is engaged in the construction and goes for solo walks in the mountains during his breaks. When he contracts pneumonia, he refuses care and continues to work. One day he does not come back from the mountains but stays there to die on the flanks of the mountain he was in awe of all his life. He passes away without glory—Whymper had taken it away from him—and without the recognition of his fellow men, who are unable to sympathize. He is later found near the Schwarzsee chapel (Maria zum Schnee), where he had once spent a cold night with Kennedy before they attempted to make a winter ascent of the Matterhorn. In the end he had lost all self-respect and strength to carry on living.

Peter Taugwalder is dead. Edward Whymper is famous. He no longer needs to fear a rival as Jean-Antoine Carrel keeps an increasingly low profile. Unable to climb a mountain without a guide and without being familiar with the tools of science, Whymper still wants to impress as a mountaineer and researcher by trying to do the impossible. The mountains remain the springboard for his fame.

Old Taugwalder's son Peter, the new "Matterhorn Peter," continues to lead tourists up the Matterhorn, reaching the summit 125 times. He marries Barbara Salzgeber, and the couple have six children. Peter never ceases to tell the dramatic story of the first ascent of the Matterhorn. He is not bitter like his father and answers curious questions, often spicing his response with sarcasm and irony. But after a falling rock smashes his knee and puts an end to his guiding career, the fifty-seven-year-old Peter is less inclined to tolerate questions about the tragedy on the Matterhorn. "Matterhorn Peter" does not need to justify himself. He has had an impressive career as a mountain guide and by now the locals know exactly what happened on the mountain in 1865. His sense of humor helps him to come to terms with his anger toward Whymper: "The Englishman portrayed my father and me as despicable companions, which is indeed a criminal defamation. . . . Here in the valley, everyone knows it and I have been told many times. Some noble men have written very good testimonies into my guidebook, which have a completely different tone from the reference Whymper gave me, without me having asked for it."

CHAPTER 36

EDWARD WHYMPER, BORN AND BRED in class-conscious Victorian England, still has an inferiority complex despite his fame and achievements as an alpinist. He may be a member of the Alpine Club, but he was not educated at Eton, Oxford, or Cambridge. He does not possess an academic title and has to work to make ends meet.

He develops grand ambitions. Nothing can top his own achievement in the Alps, but maybe he could climb the highest mountain in Europe, Mont Blanc? This is not really his goal, given the fact that several hundred people have climbed it already. Nevertheless, in 1893 he climbs it with Frédéric Payot, and the pair even pass the night on the summit. When Whymper realizes that the highest mountain in the world, which is suspected to be somewhere in the Himalayas, is financially not feasible, he concentrates his attention on the tallest mountain in the Americas. This he locates somewhere in the equatorial Andes, and he plans an expedition to go there. (It is not yet known that Aconcagua is actually the highest mountain in the New World.) Climbed peaks are of no interest to him.

Why is Whymper's fame constantly growing while Jean-Antoine Carrel's does not? The latter may not be a scientific researcher, but he is definitely the better climber.

After the tragic year of 1865, Whymper continues to visit Zermatt, resides in the Hotel Monte Rosa, and is always searching for obedient helpers. He tries his luck as a snow researcher, which slowly turns "Whymper the mountaineer" into "Whymper the scientist." The English visitors admire him for his work even though his social standing does not quite equal theirs. Any initial contempt dwindles with the success of his book, and eventually only a few of his most famous club fellows—Moore, Stephens, Tyndall, and Coolidge—still look at Whymper with skepticism. Saussure, Forbes, and Tuckett, who legitimized their Alpinist deeds with scientific research, become his idols. The mountain guides remain his underlings, just as they were on the Matterhorn between 1860 and 1865.

Whymper is now engaged in researching the metamorphosis of snow to firn and ice. Striving to gain social recognition with his glaciological research, Whymper appears on the mountain armed with shovels and drills and has shafts of twenty-two feet and twenty-six feet dug into the firn. Just as with his guides—whom he divided into good, bad, or mediocre; French, Swiss, or Italian—he demands obedience and modesty from the workers he hires. "I want good value for the francs they extract from my pocket," he later writes. While he chooses to sing the praises of his silent companions, such as his tent porter Luc, he belittles the abilities of experienced climbers.

Not all mountain people are prepared to adopt such submissive attitudes as Whymper expects, and Carrel is one of these. As a guide he was prepared to take on all responsibilities on the mountain, but he was not willing to tolerate Whymper's idiosyncrasies. With his attitude, Whymper slowly damages his credibility among the guides, although he remains in good standing in the Alpine Club. Still, Whymper's absurd accusations against old Peter are mostly left unchallenged and remain so, even after old Peter's death. And only because nobody dares to question his stamina, his storytelling, and his mountaineering experience!

As in 1867, Whymper travels to the Arctic, western Greenland, to study glaciation in 1872. But just as in 1867 he does not achieve any results. His actual goal, to discover the North Pole, is put to rest when he does not find an Inuit who is willing to take him there. Studying indigenous people and their living conditions interests him, but it does not make any money.

Thanks to his book and his engravings, Whymper basks in fame and popularity. *Scrambles Amongst the Alps* unites the arts of narration and drawing. These two talents merge in a style that is modern and traditional at the same time. And as many readers view Whymper as a model, someone who has realized dreams of freedom and adventure, the book is a huge success. Having gained modest wealth with it, Whymper has finally reached financial independence.

In the meantime, photography has reached the high mountains. John Ruskin, who experimented with mountain photography in 1850, makes the Matterhorn his motif. Hudson also documented his climbs with photography. Whymper, worried that this new medium could outshine his engravings, starts dabbling in photography. In 1874, he climbs the Matterhorn again, but this time solely to take photographs and do scientific research. His guides are Carrel and Jean-Baptiste Bich. Seventy-five teams have summited the Matterhorn by now.

The tense relationship Whymper has with guides—he still changes them frequently—also puts pressure on his relationship with Carrel, even though he has never had any bad experience with him. Carrel never compromised Whymper. On the contrary, he defended him for a long time. But it was Whymper who became the conqueror of the Matterhorn, and the Matterhorn became Whymper's mountain. Hence the Whymper Room in the Hotel Monte Rosa, the Whymper Dish in Zermatt, the Whymper Cake, and so on—"Whymper" and "Zermatt" are almost interchangeable. Old Peter Taugwalder, who brought Whymper back to safety in 1865, does not get a mention, and his son is only worth a footnote in Carl Haensel's *Struggle for the Matterhorn.*

Whymper's *Scrambles Amongst the Alps,* every new edition of which is amended with more details, makes him increasingly famous, even though he is nothing but an egomaniac. In 1865, he cut his own rope to detach himself in order to overtake Croz just below the summit—just to be the first. Or so he is said to have later told friends over a bottle of wine. So he is said to have told the bishop during confession. His deeds are not the problem, but his concealment of them is.

Chapter 37

In 1879, Whymper engages Jean-Antoine Carrel for an expedition to Ecuador and permits him to bring a second guide. This man turns out to be Jean-Antoine's cousin Louis Carrel. Both Carrels are supposed to accompany Whymper to the Andes and make the decisions on the mountain. Whymper is finally prepared to trust his guides, not only with the responsibility but also with finding solutions for strategic and logistical problems. The guides know the nature of the mountain; the Englishman knows its history. In 1802, the scientist Alexander von Humboldt reached the significant altitude of 18,370 feet (5,600 meters) on Chimborazo. He chose the village of Calpi south-southeast of Chimborazo as his starting point and believed that he and his small caravan could reach the summit and return to Calpi in one single day, with an altitude gain of 9,800 feet (3,000 meters) and a horizontal distance of 11.8 miles (19 kilometers). The ascent involved negotiating scree, rock walls, and seracs, and coping with oxygen-deprived air. The men suffered from altitude sickness and were forced to turn back. Humboldt later wrote: "My whole life I have been vain about having been among those few mortals who have risen highest in the world—I mean on the slopes of Chimborazo—and I was proud of my ascension! With a certain envy I am now looking at the revelations Webb and his partners are experiencing in the Indian mountains. I have refrained from traveling to the Himalayas as I believe that my work in America has given the English a first impulse to do more in the snowy mountains than they have done in one and a half centuries."

In 1802, the south side of Chimborazo is still an impossibility. Humboldt does not know anything about the flat north side and moves on. Humboldt's Chimborazo expedition terminated where Alpine summit bids usually begin, namely where the difficulties in rock and ice start to be terrifyingly unmanageable.

At the end of the nineteenth century, half a dozen attempts have been made to climb Chimborazo from the south, east, and north sides, and it is only in 1880 that Whymper and his two guides reach the top. On January 4, they become the first people to set foot on its summit, and they climb it again via its north-northwest ridge on July 3 of the same year. Whymper has his successful second ascent officially confirmed by his Ecuadorian companion Francisco Campaña as well as the British consul in Guayaquil. In Ecuador though, no one else believes his success. Here the first ascent of Chimborazo is still attributed to the statesman Simón Bolívar (1783–1830), even though nobody seriously believes this story. Whymper is now experiencing firsthand how long-lived such stories can be. He has started quite a lot of them himself.

On his first Chimborazo expedition, Whymper tackles the mountain from the southwest side without even looking at the other flanks. After all, this is the route Humboldt attempted it from. The cousins Carrel, whose decisions Whymper tacitly accepts on Chimborazo, are in charge of the team that is also joined by Perring, an Englishman living in Ecuador, and three muleteers. The expedition is exquisitely equipped: food provisions from Europe, Whymper's tents, fur sleeping bags, and all sorts of measuring instruments and alpinist devices. The small team leaves from the Tambo de Totorillas, west of Chimborazo, where they choose the third valley, the Vallon de Carrel, as Whymper calls it, as their starting point and climb toward the southwest ridge that separates the Thielmann from the

Trümmer Glaciers—two other names Whymper has come up with. The first camp, at about 14,375 feet (4,000 meters) is still in the valley, while the second camp at 16,664 feet (5,000 meters) is on the ridge. For a whole day, everyone in the party suffers from altitude sickness—headaches, vomiting, fatigue—before they reach the third camp at 17,000 feet (5,100 meters), above the snowline. On January 3, the guides and Whymper advance via the route that the Carrels have already explored up to an altitude of 18,500 feet (5,900 meters), while the muleteers descend to the lower camps and Perring stays at the third camp as a guard. Without having to cut steps, the three reach the foot of giant lava cliffs at the upper end of the ridge, being surrounded by hanging seracs. Suddenly a snowstorm breaks out, and heaven and hell seem to fuse. Whiteout! Whymper only survives this storm because he trusts Jean-Antoine, who just like back home, knows what to do in the Andes at 20,000 feet (6,000 meters) above sea level.

The next morning, the three men are on the move again, climbing over loose lava slopes and zigzagging across steep firn to reach the western end of the west summit. Jean-Antoine Carrel carries a heavy box containing a mercury barometer, impairing his progress on the high plateau. The snow there is so deep and loose that it has to be trudged through inch by inch. In places the men sink into fresh snow and are sometimes forced to crawl on all fours. After three hours they finally reach the slightly rounded west summit, only to realize that the south summit is actually higher. So they continue digging through the snow to reach the highest point of the mountain, where the barometer reading shows an altitude of 20,549 feet (6,262 meters), and when they hoist the Union Jack there is only an hour and a half of daylight left for the descent. The section with the soft snow requires almost as much energy on the descent, and they only reach firm ground after the sun has set. Here the three men run for their lives, hurrying to pass the difficult sections before complete darkness sets in. They get away by the skin of their teeth, stumbling across loose scree to finally reach camp at nine o'clock in the evening, exhausted from a sixteen-hour effort.

Whymper's youthful arrogance at the time of his first ascent of the Matterhorn has given way to a feeling of national obligation. He now wants to gain honor for his kingdom. Still in good physical condition, he is able to keep up with the best guides, but he now leaves leadership and responsibility on the mountain up to them. Whymper has finally turned into the traditional mountaineer he refused to be on the Matterhorn: committed to Great Britain, science, and the Alpine Club, a mountain tourist with a guide as well as the Union Jack. Now he stays at the high camp for two more days to collect moss, rocks, and plants, and he takes all sorts of measurements. However, foggy conditions impair his work, and in the end his map of Chimborazo is not precise enough to show any groundbreaking findings in snow research. His drawings of colossal blankets of firn, a storm-ravaged tent, and glacier tongues covered in rubble are as powerful as ever, though.

Half a year later, on July 3, 1880, Whymper reaches the summit of Chimborazo for the second time. This time he summits from the northwest side and in the best season. After climbing in the Andes for half a year and being acclimatized to the higher altitudes, the Carrels do not encounter any trouble in leading their protégé as well as two women from Ecuador to the summit.

Coming from Carihuairazo, Whymper pitches his tents on the north-northwest ridge, and as before, Carrel has to scout the route. On July 2, Whymper is at base camp at 15,700 feet (4,800 meters). The climbing party sets out very early the next day and reaches its goal—the south summit of Chimborazo—at 1:20 p.m. For the first time in history, Ecuadorians have reached the summit—under European leadership.

This time the snowdrift is not as bad as during their first ascent, but the dangers are of a different kind: Cotopaxi, the volcano about sixty miles to the north, has erupted. Already during the ascent, a gray dust cloud from the northeast obscured the sky. On the summit, the falling ashes are so thick that the climbers can hardly make out the west summit, which is very close. They quickly take their barometer readings and start their descent, where they find the path and the upper camps covered in ash.

Once again Whymper did not accomplish anything in researching mountain nature. His collections of rocks, plants, and insects from the higher regions barely complement those of other researchers. Nevertheless, he uses his research to justify his expeditions in public, as this natural science seems to be more important to him than the nature of human beings. Whymper now sees himself as a researcher, not the conqueror of the Matterhorn, but he still has not learned how to take responsibility on the mountain. Without reservation he leaves the responsibility to the loyal Jean-Antoine Carrel. He has now become the epitome of a Victorian conqueror. As unfair as he was to the Taugwalders after the Matterhorn tragedy, he has now adjusted to the current conditions. The only thing important to him is the way he is perceived.

In the midst of this Andean expedition, during which the guides repeatedly save things from deteriorating if not from total disaster, Carrel and Whymper have their final falling out. The Englishman lacks sufficient empathy to understand why Carrel feels responsible for him. Old Taugwalder had reacted similarly in Whymper's presence. Both guides saw in Whymper a big child who needed to be looked after.

Later in life, Whymper becomes cantankerous, bitter, and quiet. He marries late and then divorces. His daughter from this marriage, Ethel Whymper, will traverse the Matterhorn from Zermatt to Breuil in 1930.

Edward Whymper, who spends the last years of his life in Chamonix, has just returned there from Zermatt when he falls ill in 1911. He locks himself up in his hotel room, refuses any medical help, and dies—just as alone as old Peter Taugwalder—on August 16, 1911, aged seventy-one.

Chapter 38

Twenty-five years after the first ascent of the Matterhorn, on August 21, 1890, the Italian composer Leone Sinigaglia, member of the Turin section of the CAI, engages two mountain guides in Courmayeur to climb the Matterhorn. One of the guides happens to be the aging Jean-Antoine Carrel, who has just returned from Mont Blanc, and the other is Charles Gorret, also from Valtournenche. Under their guidance, Sinigaglia intends to traverse the Matterhorn. Carrel, who is supposed to lead the expedition, has heard from other mountain guides that the conditions on the mountain are phenomenally good: dry rock, firm snow, clear skies.

On the eve of August 22, the men reach Breuil. The valley basin is green, it is warm, and the Matterhorn towers black against a bright evening sky. There is not a breath in the air, the bells of the grazing animals are ringing, and there are only a few snowy patches to be seen on the mountain. It is here that Whymper started his expedition a quarter of a century earlier.

At quarter past two in the morning, the three head out. The skies continue clear, with the stars over the Matterhorn pointing them in the right direction, but the mountain's silhouette seems eerie. Sinigaglia intends to reach the summit via the Italian ridge in one day and descend into Switzerland all the way down to the Hörnli Hut. But Carrel takes his time, acts carefully, and tries not to overstretch his client's abilities. Or can he sense the impending change in the weather? He breathes in the fresh morning air, stops more often than necessary, and looks toward the summit.

Sinigaglia and Gorret notice that Carrel is fatigued. Very slowly he leads the way up to the Col du Lion, his movements almost dragging, as if climbing is more exhausting for him than usual. The increasingly oppressive atmosphere does not help either. Since sunrise, mist has been creeping up the south face, like smoke rising from the underworld. Again and again Carrel stops and turns around, as if carrying a rucksack as well as responsibility is a bigger burden than usual. When the party reaches the Gran Torre Hut at half past ten, they meet a few guides who are on their way down. They have repaired the fixed rope in places. "Have a good climb," they say. Carrel decides to postpone the summit attempt to the next day. "Here we can recover a bit," he says.

Nobody objects, partly because dark clouds have now gathered. One by one the men squeeze through the narrow door into the tiny wooden hut at the base of the Great Tower.

Carrel lies down and sleeps for a few hours. When he wakes up and hears the storm rattling on the roof of the hut, he is worried. He gesticulates, his white beard moving up and down as if he wants to explain something. But he says nothing, and his deep-set eyes have almost disappeared.

Confined in the gloomy darkness of the hut, fear creeps in. The men are protected from the snow, but the wind blows through the cracks, rattles the door, whistles around the corners. Both windows facing the valley are covered in snow. Nothing can be seen.

Hunched over and clad in his black, woolen clothes, Carrel slowly feels his way to the door. When he opens it slightly, pieces of ice and snow whirl through the hut, accompanied by an eerie roar, and he quickly closes it.

Sinigaglia and Gorret crouch on the bench facing the mountain side of the hut when Carrel opens the door a second time—this time far enough to peer outside. But he cannot see a thing. No steps, no rock, not even snow: a vast nothing is right outside the door. It looks like the only thing left is an abyss on all sides—and the power of the storm.

"No earth, no sky," Gorret and Sinigaglia hear the old man mumble. He pushes the door closed with both hands, lies down again, and keeps silent. For forty hours. What should he say, anyway? They are prisoners, victims of the mountain, without any hope of rescue. Just like at the high camp on Chimborazo, like with Whymper on the Matterhorn, like on Mont Blanc in the storm. Sinigaglia now knows that higher up it must be like Dante's hell: frost, thirst, hunger, and fear. Soon the inferno will reach them.

On the morning of August 25, they decide to retreat. Provisions and wood are gone; they have even burned the wooden benches. There is no way for them to melt any more snow. The weather remains atrocious, although the storm has slightly abated.

Carrel knows what needs to be done. He must—he will—take his entrusted client to safety. And if need be, *only* him, Sinigagalia. Get up for the descent!

It is not a ritual. It is an ordeal. Their clothes are frozen stiff, their throats are dry, and their blood is almost frozen.

At nine o'clock in the morning, the three leave the deceptive protection of the hut. Gorret, now in the lead, tumbles over about a dozen rock steps covered with new snow and lands in a snowfield. He does not see what he is standing on. Carrel gives him directions from above. The loose rocks below the snow cover start sliding and Gorret falls over. Flailing, attached to a rope that has tightened, the guide gets up in waist-high snow. He looks helpless, as if he is out of his depth struggling with loose snow and rocks.

Carrel doesn't panic. He knows the difficulties and dangers they will face on the descent via the steep ridge down to the Col du Lion. This will be a challenging climb. The three men have a hard day ahead. They have to deal with stiff, frozen ropes, rocks varnished with ice and then covered with snow, iced-over handholds that are difficult to find, and abysses everywhere. Carrel is at the tail end, making sure the party is safe on the rope and guiding them down step by step. The two men in front follow the order of the old guide directing them—"Left!" "Right!" "Straight down!" Wherever necessary he lowers them down vertical sections, then descends behind them.

He knows that he must not slip or fall, no matter how icy the rock is. He is responsible. Despite only seeing his contours, Carrel continues to direct Gorret, who is unable to identify any landmarks. Only in places where the rock is overhanging can they see dark spots and assess where they are. The abyss below seems bottomless. Step by step, the two guides help their client descend the mountain.

The party keeps the same order: the young guide in front, Sinigaglia in the middle, and Carrel at the end. It is only due to instinct, extreme caution, Carrel's familiarity with the route, and maybe Gorret's ability to keep a cool head that they safely reach the Col du Lion. Their clothes, soaked with snow and sweat, smell moldy. Shivering and short of breath, with wet hands and numb feet, as if they had turned into blocks of ice, they shuffle across to the black rocks of the Tete du Lion.

Carrel, who was hoping that they would find protection from the blizzard farther down on the south side of the mountain, where the winds are not as violent, is exhausted and hypothermic. His eyes are almost blind from searching for holds and looking into the void. On the col the storm flares up again, this time with a vengeance. The traverse and the rock bands below the Lion Ridge are ghastly, even though the terrain is flatter. The fresh snow on the rock steps is knee-deep, the layered rock tiles are icy, and the vertically sloping snow gullies avalanche-prone. The cold is more biting than in winter. The trio almost suffocates in the storm, their breath blown away. The gales that now seem to come from all directions are so strong that the men are afraid they will be blown off the mountain. Wind-drifted snow coats their beards, eyebrows, and mouths. With their garments laden with wet snow, the three men look as if they are wearing armor. Their hands are frozen and increasingly unusable. Having lost a glove, Gorret is unable to grip the rock with his bare hand, which has been reduced to a claw. He can only guess where to put it. Carrel is also fighting the wind and the cold. His face looks almost frighteningly old. Repeatedly he picks the ice from his eyelashes to be able to see. His beard is covered in icicles.

"Down!" he croaks.

"How?"

"On a tight rope!"

"Hold me!"

"What's happening?"

"Lower me farther."

"Only fifteen feet of rope left!"

'Hold me! I'm falling!"

"Yes! No!"

"Anchor!"

Sinigaglia does not understand a word. To him, Gorret, who is breaking trail, and Carrel, who is giving directions, are shouting in some kind of secret language. The guides make animal noises, which turn into screams and grunts. Sinigaglia does not understand their gestures either, but he trusts his guides. In the blizzard it is impossible to converse. And they have not been able to see anything for hours.

"What shall we do?" Sinigaglia shouts.

"Survive!" Gorret answers.

How else should the guides react when the future has been reduced to isolated moments, each of which is a lifetime in itself?

Carrel directs this descent miraculously: without hesitating, with inexhaustible stamina, and with the skills of a blind person's guide. He never takes his eyes off the other two men, who must not see his doubts. As if he had reached the prime of his life again, he encourages his guest and pats Sinigaglia on the shoulder every time he reaches the anchor. Sinigaglia cannot comprehend how the tired old man in the hut could have turned into such an able and stalwart guide, but it gives him courage to live. Gorret supports the older man as much as he can, partly because he knows that he would be unable to find the way back to the valley on his own. Carrel does not utter a word of discouragement or lament. He just continues to shout short commands—"Left!" "Right!" "Traverse!"—with the undying sound of the storm raging in the background.

Every once in a while, Carrel's dark figure emerges like a shadow from the storm, only to disappear again. This figure is not pushy but acts with determination. There is no sitting down, no stopping, no hesitation. Resting could be fatal now.

"Down!"

The descent is now unexpectedly dangerous. The gullies are filled with snow ready to avalanche, and Carrel's route-finding skills deteriorate as it gets darker. Even though he knows the Matterhorn like nobody else, the terrain, drifts, and mist confuse him. He hesitates more and more often and slowly inches his way forward from rock to rock, as if he were following a ghost. Are there any signs? Yes, they are on the right track still. He knows that he would be able to get himself down from anywhere. But will he be able to get the others down?

At around eleven o'clock at night, Carrel falls for the first time. Completely dehydrated, his heavy clothes soaked, covered in snow, and dead-tired, a massive shiver runs through his body. The snowstorm is still raging. His heart is racing, and he can hardly breathe. Has his heart just stopped beating for a second? Carrel knows he has reached the end. He needs to sit down. Sitting down, almost frozen to death, his hands numb, the rope as stiff as a stick, he lowers Sinigaglia across the last rocks on the way down. He has stopped feeling anything. He only knows that his hands are holding the rope. It is his duty. But what is happening to his heart? Yes, it is his heart! It beats irregularly. The safety of the chalets on the pastures below is only a stone throw away. Carrel can see the darkness of the grassy ground beyond the storm. Only a few minutes away, about 150 feet farther down, is the end of the snow line.

Carrel wants to stay there, rest, sleep. At least for the rest of the night. But what if Gorret gets lost? How often has Carrel called him back, just in time to prevent him from falling down or stepping into an avalanche gully and fatal slide. The weather is not improving. He must not die—not yet. Remaining aware to keep Gorret on the right path, Carrel stays awake. Unthinkable what would happen if the others tumbled down into the night without him. The skies above them no longer exist, climbing up is no longer an option, and safety lies down in the valley. The only way to reach it is to continue down the gully through the storm. His stubbornness and excellent instinct allow him to find exactly the gully they climbed up three days earlier. This ditch will take them to safety, to the last snowfield just above the pastures of Riondé. They take a short rest in a little cave, each of them having a sip of cognac.

Then they continue down. But Carrel falls behind on the traverse of the last snowfield. The rope leading to Sinigaglia becomes tight, and it remains so for a while. "Why is he so slow?" Sinigaglia asks himself. He turns around but is unable to hear or see the guide.

Carrel has collapsed behind a rock, landing first on his knees before slumping to the ground.

Gorret calls back to him: "What's up?"

"Nothing!" Carrel manages to blurt.

"Why is the rope so tight?"

"It's nothing," Carrel repeats.

He gets up slowly and looks around. Yes, he knows where they are and what he needs to do now. He continues slowly, firmly holding onto the rope. Have the other two already reached the pastures? He stops again and looks around.

"We are down!" Gorret calls out.

Carrel is no longer able to speak or hear. Gorret and Sinigaglia are still attached to the rope leading to Carrel. Carrel follows their tracks on all fours, tries to get up again to make sure the others have reached safety. Gorret is already walking across the grass as if he has taken over the lead. The rope has become redundant.

In the last snowfield, from which a short but steep grassy gully leads to the safety of the pastures of Riondé, Carrel feels dizzy again. He sways and sits. He is dead tired from staring into the blankness of the fog, from shivering in the cold, from securing the others, and from the burden of the responsibility, which he has carried until this moment. Feeling close to safety, Gorret continues to descend the grassy slope, step by step, in the lead. Sinigaglia follows him on a long rope. But where is Carrel? Gorret has almost reached the pastures when he feels a tug on the rope, which also jolts Sinigaglia. Both men stop and call back, but Carrel no longer responds, and he does not appear.

"Jean-Antoine!" Gorret calls into the night.

Nothing.

"Come!"

Sinigaglia also shouts up to Carrel, telling him to come down, as they no longer need the security of his rope. No reply. Worried, Gorret goes back up the slope a few steps. Only now can he hear Carrel's voice: "I have no strength left."

But where is he? Moving along the rope, Gorret struggles up the slope, closely followed by Sinigaglia.

With great effort the two men manage to get back to the guide. When they find him he is covered in hard snow, clenching a rock, completely and utterly exhausted. But even though he is unable to get up, let alone continue to descend, he seems content.

"Enough," he says. "You can fetch me later."

Gorret and Sinigaglia pull his limp body to a flat spot. Gorret wants to ask Carrel something but is unable to utter a word.

"What is wrong with him?" Sinigaglia wants to know.

Gorret just stares blindly into the stormy sky.

"He is dying," Sinigaglia whispers.

"I don't know," Carrel says, his voice a croak.

"We are almost down," Gorret says.

"Where?"

"In Riondé."

"And where am I?" Carrel wonders.

Carrel's hands are white and cold, his breath flat, his body limp.

Gorret pours the last bit of white wine into the mouth of the dying man. He then gives him some cognac, also the last of it. Carrel groans, turns around, and tries to get on his hands and knees.

"You are down," he suddenly says with certainty, then slumps back into the snow.

Gorret attempts to get him up and rubs his face with snow, but this is in vain. Carrel is no longer able to respond except to moan. Lifting him is impossible. Gorret holds his head, presses his mouth against his ear and asks him if he wishes to commend his soul to God.

"I want to thank."

"God?"

"For the strength."

"To do your duty?" asks Gorret.

"Yes."

Sinigaglia understands as little—and as much—from these last words as he did when Carrel was shouting rope commands. He only knows that he would be dead without the instincts of his guide.

Carrel wheezes, followed by a deep and long exhalation: a noise as if his body were now emptied and hollowed. Gorret lets go of Carrel's head. The guide lies on his back in the snow, his empty eyes directed toward the sky where the moon now appears through the clouds.

"Get up!" Gorret shouts at Sinigaglia, who is just about to go to sleep. "We will freeze to death if we stop here!" They must not lose any more time. They cut the rope between them and Carrel—the rope that saved their lives while descending from the mountain to the valley —and continue back down, leaving the man who did not allow them to die. The guide who returned his team to safety and then perished at the foot of the mountain.

Gorret and Sinigalia continue to walk through the night. The only way to keep from freezing is to keep moving. Hurrying down toward safety, they reach the inn in Giomein at five o'clock in the morning, completely exhausted. They have been on their feet for twenty hours, without food or rest, constantly fearing for their lives. The proprietor is awake. Apparently there has been great concern about the missing climbers.

Six men, the mountain guides Alessandro Pession, Elia Pession, and Vittorio Maquignaz from Valtournenche, and three local herders head out to recover Carrel's body. Two Swiss mountain guides, Schaller and Pollinger, join the group later. During the descent more and more people join the procession.

Down in the valley others observe through binoculars. The men carrying Carrel's body are in the lead. It is like a procession down from heaven.

The news of Carrel's heroic death spreads fast. Villagers are shocked and fall into deep grief. "It was God's will," consoles Abbé Gorret, now the village priest.

Leone Sinigaglia will remember: "Carrel died, like a good and brave man, on his own mountain, after having summoned all the energy he possessed in order to save his employer. He died after bringing him out of danger to a place of safety, exhausted by the supreme effort of sixteen hours of assiduous work, amid continuous struggles and difficulties, in a snowstorm which several times appeared irresistible. I shall never think of him without infinite emotion and gratitude."

Carrel's body is taken to the chapel in Giomein, where it is displayed for three days.

On August 29, Carrel's remains are taken to Valtournenche and buried in the graveyard of the village, with the Matterhorn towering like a statue against the brilliant sky.

EPILOGUE

IN 1890, THE YEAR OF Carrel's death, a businessman approached the Swiss government in Bern asking for permission to build a railroad from Zermatt to the Gornergrat and another one from Zermatt all the way to the top of the Matterhorn. The media soon reported on construction plans, and the line to the Gornergrat was indeed built and has been operating since 1899. The plan to construct the other one has fortunately never come to fruition, but the brainchild of the Swiss engineer Xaver Imfeld lives on in the imagination, at least. The latter envisages construction of a line to the Hörnli Ridge, from which a straight tunnel of about two kilometers would be hammered into the mountain and end just below the summit on the Zmutt side.

Five years after Jean-Antoine Carrel's death, Edward Whymper visited Breuil one last time, in August 1895, and climbed the Carrel route halfway to the summit to take photographs, advancing to the base of the Great Tower via the southwest ridge. In *Scrambles Amongst the Alps*, he adds:

> More than thirty years had elapsed since my last visit, and I found
> that great changes had taken place in the interval. The summit of the
> Col du Lion was lower than it was formerly, from diminution of the
> snow; and the passage across it was shorter than it used to be. For
> the next 150 feet or so of ascent there was little alteration, but thence
> upwards the ridge had tumbled to pieces, and many familiar places
> were unrecognizable. No spot on this ridge is more firmly fixed in my
> recollection than "the Chimney"; only a remnant of it was left and

more than half of the Chimney had disappeared; and from that point upwards everything was altered.

Difficult places had become easy, and easy places had become difficult. The angle in which a thick, knotted rope is now dangling, which is now one of the steepest bits of the ascent, did not exist in 1864.

Today there are fixed ropes and even ladders on both sides of the Matterhorn, the Lion Ridge and the Hörnli Ridge. These make the Horu—or Gran Becca, if you prefer—accessible to those who do not have the technical skills to scale it otherwise. It is very similar to Mount Everest, where Sherpas fix the lines for the masses of tourists. Both have become commercial mountains.

The 1865 "struggle for the Matterhorn" marked the beginning of this development, which radically changed mountaineering from striving to conquer to proving one's technical climbing abilities. And both Matterhorn pioneers Whymper and Carrel have become symbolic figures for it. However, when it comes to the triumph over the Matterhorn, only Whymper's name seems to be remembered: the young lad, as tall as the mountain, who was the first person to climb it. To this day, Whymper is still famous as a pioneer, admired as a painter, and read as an author. There is no doubt that he was a reasonable mountaineer with noble ideals and goals. He just refused to take responsibility for his actions.

TRANSLATOR'S NOTE

HOW DID I END UP translating a book about the Matterhorn, a mountain I have never climbed and only set eyes on a few years ago? It was a mountain I knew very little about other than from having visited the impressive Matterhorn Museum in Zermatt, Switzerland. A mountain many historians, researchers, and mountaineers have written about, still trying to get rid of some of its demons. A mountain everyone seems to associate with the English mountaineer Edward Whymper and, of course, the disaster that happened on his descent in 1865.

When I agreed to translate Reinhold Messner's latest book for Mountaineers Books I had no idea how much insight I would glean about the rivalry between the Italian climber Jean-Antoine Carrel and the British climber Edward Whymper, about the way the English viewed the Italian and Swiss peasants in the nineteenth century, and about the fate that finally befell Carrel, who scaled the Matterhorn without incident three days after Whymper's team reached the peak, on July 17, 1865.

The process of translating this book piqued my curiosity to find out more about the ill-fated first ascent of the Matterhorn, and I was amazed by how much literature there was, by the vast number of journals in the archives of the Alpine Club, as well as the abundance of newspaper articles that were—and still are—questioning Whymper's abilities and his responsibilities. These questions must have been on Reinhold Messner's mind for many years, and he took the occasion of the 150th anniversary of the Matterhorn's first ascent to write down his view of the events that unfolded in July 1865. Messner has dug deep into the history of the climb, put himself into Carrel's shoes, and scrutinized Whymper's *Scrambles Amongst the Alps*. Another great book Messner has drawn from is Alan Lyall's *The First Descent of the Matterhorn: A Bibliographical Guide to the 1865 Accident and Its Aftermath*, which has been described as the bible of the Matterhorn.

The hero in this book is Jean-Antoine Carrel, a man hardly anyone has heard of as he did not succeed in beating Whymper to the top. But who actually knows the second men to scale Mount Everest? Most will have heard of Sir Edmund Hillary and Sherpa Tenzing Norgay, but who knows the names of Jürg Marmet and Ernst Schmied from Switzerland, who were the third and fourth persons to stand on top of the world three years after the first ascent? This is a fact of life: the first counts; the second falls into oblivion. This reminds me of my work for the expedition archives of Elizabeth Hawley. When the Himalayan chronicler first started collecting mountaineering information in 1963, most expeditions represented attempted firsts: the first to summit, the first to reach the top from a certain nation, the first woman, and so on. However, it has become rather difficult to be the first of anything these days, so some of the climbers have come up with the most absurd ideas of how to scale an 8,000-meter peak: be it with a bicycle, without arms or legs, in their underpants, as a diabetic, as a vegan, as the first married couple, et cetera.

Every year between 2,500 and 3,000 people attempt to climb the Matterhorn, and just as with Everest, times have changed. Even though the spirits of Whymper and Carrel are still somewhere on the flanks of the mountain, scaling it has become very possible for more average mortals, who are unaware of the great myths that surrounded the Matterhorn before its first ascent. For this reason, Messner's book is a great reminder of what mountaineering used to be like. Even though the motives were different back then, rivalry already existed.

I would like to thank Mountaineers Books for giving me the chance to translate this captivating and revealing story into English, Suzy Conway and Elizabeth Hawley for proofreading and improving my English in places, Ed Douglas for helping me out and finding the original versions of some of the letters that were written in English, and my friends and family for bearing with me over the last six months and understanding that I was completely engrossed in this book. I hope you have enjoyed reading it as much as I enjoyed translating it.

Billi Bierling
Kathmandu, September 2016

SOURCES

Alpen, Die. Zietschrift des Schwizer Alpen-Clubs. (*Swiss Alpine Journal*)

Alpine Journal, The. The Alpine Club.

Braunstein, Josef: "Zur Ersteigungsgeschichte des Matterhorns" in *Alpenfreund*, 1925.

Dangar, D.F.O. and T.S. Blakeney: *The Matterhorn Centenary. The Alpine Journal*, Vol 70, 1965.

Fantin, Mario. *Cervino 1865–1965.* Bologna, Italy: Tamari Editori, 1965.

Gorret, Amé. "Die erst Begehung des italienischen Grates"in *Deutsche Alpenzeitung*, Vol. 27, 1932.

Gos, Charles. *Le Cervin: L'epoque Héroïque 1857–1867.* Corcelles, Switzerland: Editions Victor Attinger, 1948.

Grosjean, Georges. "Die Erstebesteigung des Matterhorns am 14, July 1865" in *Die Alpen*, 1965.

Kronig, Stanislaus. *Familien-Statistik und Geschichtliches über die Gemeinde Zermatt, 1927.* Zermatt: Neue Buchdr. Visp, 1982.

Lunn, Arnold and Albert Bettex. "Taugwalder und das Matterhorn" in *Du*, June 1946.

Lyall, Alan. *The First Descent of the Matterhorn: A Bibliographical Guide to the 1865 Accident & Its Aftermath.* Ceredigion, Wales: Gomer Press, 1997.

Mazzotti, Giuseppe. *Das Buch vom Matterhorn.* Berlin, Germany: Union Deutsche Verlagsgesellschaft, 1935.

Meissner, Alfred in *Neue Freie Press Wien*, Nr. 336, 4 August 1865.

Perren, Luisa and Beat Perren. *Cervino, La gran becca.* Anzola d'Ossola, Italy: Fondazione Enrico Monti, 2009.

Rey, Guido. *Das Matterhorn*. Oberhaching, Germany: Bergverlag Rother, 1959.

Sinigaglia, Leone. "La morte di Giovanni Antonio Carrel" in *Revista mensil del CAI*, 30 August 1890.

Taugwalder, Hannes and Martin Jaggi. *Der Wahrheit näher: Die Katastrophe am Matterhorn 1865 und andere Erstbesteigungen*. Aarau, Switzerland: Glendyn Verlag, 1990.

Viriglio, A. *Jean Antoine Carrel*. Bologna: Licinio Cappelli Editore, 1956.

Whymper, Edward. *The Ascent of the Matterhorn*. London: John Murray, 1880.

————. Letter to *The Times*, 8 August 1865.

————. *Scrambles Amongst the Alps in the Years 1860–69*, 4th edition. London: John Murray, 1893.

————. *Travels Amongst the Great Andes of the Equator*. London: John Murray, 1893.

Williams, Cicely. *Zermatt: Geschichte und Geschichten*. Brig, Switzerland: Rotten-Verlag, 1964.

ABOUT THE AUTHOR

REINHOLD MESSNER, BORN IN 1944 in Villnöss South Tyrol, is the most famous mountaineer and adventurer of our time. He has accomplished about one hundred first ascents, climbed all fourteen eight-thousanders, and crossed the Antarctic, Greenland, Tibet, and the Gobi and Takla Makan deserts on foot.

After serving a term as a member of the European Parliament, he now devotes much of his time and energy to his Messner Mountain Museum project and to his foundation, the Messner Mountain Foundation, which aims to support mountain people worldwide. For more about the author, visit www.reinhold-messner.de.

MOUNTAINEERS BOOKS, including its two imprints, Skipstone and Braided River, is a leading publisher of quality outdoor recreation, sustainability, and conservation titles. As a 501(c)(3) nonprofit, we are committed to supporting the environmental and educational goals of our organization by providing expert information on human-powered adventure, sustainable practices at home and on the trail, and preservation of wilderness.

Our publications are made possible through the generosity of donors, and through sales of more than 800 titles on outdoor recreation, sustainable lifestyle, and conservation. To donate, purchase books, or learn more, visit us online:

MOUNTAINEERS BOOKS

1001 SW Klickitat Way, Suite 201 • Seattle, WA 98134
800-553-4453 • mbooks@mountaineersbooks.org • www.mountaineersbooks.org

THE LEGENDS AND LORE SERIES honors the lives and adventures of mountaineers and is made possible in part through the generosity of donors. Mountaineers Books, a nonprofit publisher, further contributes to this investment through book sales from more than 800 titles on outdoor recreation, sustainable lifestyle, and conservation.

We would like to thank the following for their charitable support of Legends and Lore:

FOUNDERS CIRCLE
- Anonymous
- Tina Bullitt
- Tom and Kathy Hornbein
- Dianne Roberts and Jim Whittaker
- William Sumner
- Doug and Maggie Walker

With special appreciation to Tom Hornbein, who donates to the series all royalties earned through the sale of his book, Everest: The West Ridge.

You can help us preserve and promote mountaineering literature by making a donation to the Legends and Lore series. For more information, benefits of sponsorship, or how you can support future work, please contact us at mbooks@mountaineersbooks.org or visit us online at www.mountaineersbooks.org.

MOUNTAINEERS
BOOKS